We Survived Iraq and Turkey
Long Road to Freedom

A True Story of an Iraqi Kurdish Family's
Escape to America

(New Version)
2017

Author
Taha M. Muhammad

Editor
Mr. Orlo Otteson

1

NOTE

Dear Reader:

I published three previous versions of my story. I was unfamiliar at the time with book publishing methods in the U.S.

I have incorporated material from these three previous books into the latest book titled *We Survived Iraq and Turkey*, and I have added new material to that version. I have cancelled contracts with the companies that published the three previous books under the following titles:

1) *Mr. Muhammad Survives Iraq: Long Road to Freedom.*
2) *Struggle for America: Lilly's Grandpa's True Story.*
3- Night Kite: A True Story of an Iraqi Family's Escape to America.

I apologize if this has caused any confusion to any readers. I think the latest version provides a fuller account of my family's experience, and I hope the reader will find it rewarding. I hope you enjoy reading my book—*We Survived Iraq and Turkey: Long Road to Freedom.*

Author: Taha M. Muhammad

Table of Contents

PREFACE

My name is Taha Muhammad. I am a Kurd from Iraqi Kurdistan, now residing in Lonsdale, Minnesota, a small community approximately thirty miles south of the Twin Cities. My wife's name is Malika Muhammad. Our sons are Yousif, Cameron, Saman, and Rezgar. Our story, however, is rooted in Kurdish history; and it begins in Kirkuk, Iraq, a city and a region with a rich and tangled history.

My purpose in writing the book was several fold:

1- To tell my story—both my life in Iraq and my escape to freedom.

2- To provide a brief history of Iraqi Kurds.

3- To relate Saddam Hussein's brutal oppression of the Kurds and to give voice to the thousands who now lie buried in mass graves (in 1983 and 1988), and died by Saddam's Chemical Kurdish Genocide in Halabja city.

4- To recount the story of my family's escape from oppression and fear.

5- To acknowledge those who helped us find a home in America.

6- To inform my grandchildren about some of their family history, so that they better understand the family's origin and fully value their American freedom.

6

7- To inform young Americans about the great benefits of being American—freedom, excellent education system, health care, good transportation systems, wonderful people, and myriad other advantages.

A word about me

I grew up and resided in Kirkuk, in the northern and Kurdish part of Iraq, a rugged region that is populated by Kurds, but whose original inhabitants included Turkmen, Chaldeans, and Assyrians. I do not consider myself an Iraqi and neither an Arab or Persian—and I sure as am not a Mountain Turk, as the Turks like to think of us. Kurds around the world, including historians and other scholars, scoff at the Turkish view that we don't exist as a distinct people and that we are "Mountain Turks."

My mother was a housewife, and my father was a small shop owner. I grew up with four brothers and two sisters, in a culturally diverse neighborhood in which both Kurds and Turkmen resided. My native language is neither Arabic nor Turkish—it is Kurdish. I am a Kurd, and better yet, I am an American Kurd. I am fluent in Kurdish, and also fluent in the Turkmen dialect of the Turkish language. My K-12 education was delivered in Arabic, and thus I can speak, read, and write in Arabic.

Living under Saddam Hussein's oppressive Ba'ath regime was an unhappy and highly limiting experience. We were denied educational and economic opportunities, and Iraqi Arab propaganda was shoved down our throats from all directions. We lived in fear; as we watched the Iraqi army burn Kurdish villages and the Saddam Hussein thugs imprison innocent Kurds.

Even before the arrival of Hussein's Ba'ath regime, our family endured some terrible suffering at the hands of other security apparatuses, of previous regimes. The Turkmen and Iraqi Government's mafia shot and killed my oldest brother a day before I was scheduled to take my final ninth grade exams. At age eleven, my oldest son was struck and killed by a vehicle while riding his bicycle. The driver was an Arab from the south, one of those that Hussein had imported to reduce the influence of the Kurds in Kirkuk. The driver was not licensed to operate a motor vehicle, and he was arrested, tried, and sentenced. Five weeks later, he was spotted in Kirkuk— a free man and driving a vehicle. Two of my cousins were sent to the gallows, a punishment for defending Kurdish rights.

These tragic experiences profoundly affected me and my family members. I began to seek ways to get my family to safety. I tried eight times to leave the country, and failed each time.

In 1990, Saddam invaded Kuwait. This time his secret police thugs not only harassed me but also came after my sons. They would periodically appear at my door and demand that I and my two oldest sons join the Iraqi military forces—and go to Kuwait and fight the Americans. They even detained my second oldest son age 18, Cam, for a day, when they could not locate me.

This incident, along with others, made me even more determined to escape—to get my family members to a safe place. That opportunity came on November 9, 1990, when we found a passage to Turkey, making our way through the mountainous terrain of Iraqi Kurdistan with the help of Kurdish smugglers. Once inside Turkey, we did not find the expected relief. We faced constant threats of expulsion and a return to Iraq.

We continued our long journey in Turkey, and ultimately came into contact with the U.S. Marines, a blessed turn of events that allowed us to gain eventual refugee status in America—instead of being returned to Iraq, where we knew we would face the deadly wrath of the Ba'ath regime.

Once in America, I began to feel the inner peace that had long eluded me. Some years later, I joined U.S. military as a civilian linguist to rebuild Iraq.

I am a graduate of the University of Baghdad in Iraq, with a degree in mathematics. Three years after my arrival in America, I earned a bachelor's degree in mathematics from Minot State University in Minot, North Dakota, and a master's degree in mathematics from the University of North Dakota. I then taught mathematics in public schools in Montana. After five years my wife and I obtained U.S. citizenship. After six years I acquired my first house. My sons hold degrees in pharmacy, international studies, and computer science. I am proud to be an American Kurd. I have published books, and I write regularly to American presidents and senators, expressing my views and opinions.

If you are wondering why I wanted to move my family out of Iraq, away from the brutal Saddam regime, the note below, written by my son Yousif may help explain my motivation.

In 1986, after I finished the exams for the 10th grade, the regime of Saddam Hussein ordered every student who was in the 10th and 11th grade to serve for one month of the summer vacation in the Iraqi Army. I went to school to pick up my grades for the 10th grade, but the principal of school, who was a member of Saddam's Ba'ath's regime, would not give me my grades. He said that I had to go serve or face the consequences of failing and serving in Saddam's Army without limit. Other students and I attending the same grade were put on a small bus and taken to a Baath center, after which we were taken to an army base two hours from Kirkuk city. They did not even notify our parents of our transfer. I was 15 years of age at that point. We were given no food for the first night, but we did get our evil uniforms. I call them evil because they were the same uniforms worn by those who killed so many thousands of innocent Kurdish people. I had no choice but to wear it. We felt like chickens in a cage.

At four o'clock in the morning we were wakened up. We had to go for a run on empty and hungry stomachs. Then they trained us and disciplined us on the greatness of the Iraqi Army and Saddam's regime. Three hours after that they would serve us breakfast. There were about one hundred students in the group. We were served cheese, tea, and bread. The bread was so hard and solid that one could use it as a hammer and not as a food to eat. The dining hall consisted of ten tables. Those in charge would put ten students at each table and bring one small tray of food for each table. We entered and stood by our table; no chairs were provided so we had to eat standing. Anyone who disobeyed any order would be punished and would not be allowed to eat. When the order was given, the students attacked the tray, and sometimes I ended up with little or no food at all. We were given five minutes to finish our food. Sometimes, before we started eating, the officer responsible for giving the order to eat would approach each tray and spit in it. The students were so hungry that the spit was a minor thing. After breakfast, we had one hour to relax, take a nap, or do whatever. Then we would gather again for the afternoon session.

The summer season in Iraq is a killer one. Temperatures can reach 120 Fahrenheit some times. Again we would go jogging. This is very hard especially while carrying a AK-47 machine gun. So many students fainted or passed out. There were even incidents during which an average of five to ten students died each summer. I was one of the lucky survivors. After our hardcore training we would go to the dining hall for lunch, and it was the same story with the distribution of food. Then we would relax for a couple of hours before going back again on the field to march, jog, train on weapons such as the AK-47, hand guns, bazookas, and hand grenades, and of course receive more instruction about the evil Baath Party. This was the routine for the whole month except for the last two days when we would go and shoot targets. I guess they were training us for the future. I did this evil training three times: at 10th grade, 11th grade, and the first year of college. Each time when I came back home I would have lost 10-15 pounds. These were truly some of the worst times of my entire life.

I had to do the training in the army for the third time when I was in my first year of college. I was 18 by then. When we got to the base, I was thinking of playing a game on the authorities and faking that I was sick. On the first day of training after jogging for one hour we gathered, and I pretended that I fainted. The leader of my group, probably a sergeant, ordered a couple of students to carry me and put me in a shade somewhere. I knew what was happening around me, and, to be frank with you, I was really enjoying the shade. Two hours later everyone in my group, especially the students that I knew, rushed toward me because they truly thought something was wrong with me. A couple of them thought that I could no longer breathe and that I needed CPR. One student was compressing my chest, and the other was pouring water on me. They both had no clue what CPR was, and I was enjoying myself and laughing so hard inside. Ten minutes later, the ambulance came and took me to the hospital. A couple of nurses came toward me, and I could hear them were talking to me. I was not responding and pretended like I had a seizure. One of the nurses came too close and sprayed something in my nostril, which was a very sharp, burning perfume. When the nurse did that, he went towards my leg, and I kicked him on his chest while my eyes were open. He landed on the ground, and his friends laughed at him. Then I was brought into the hospital and was given a panic attack injection. I woke up three hours later, and they told me that I had a panic attack. Well, I guess my plan was successful for one day. They gave me a break for one day and resumed training the day after.

Another thing that I remember is that we would be forced out of school and made to go to the streets carry slogans and praise Saddam dictator. All road and gates were closed and anyone that tried to escape from the demonstration would be severely punished and tortured".

Note: The above was my simple statement for my father's humble book.
Yousif T. Murad

Acknowledgments
We owe our lives to members of the U.S. Marine Corp, specifically Lt. Baker, Sergeant Vick, and Colonel James Jones—who later became commandant of the Marine Corps, NATO commander in Europe, and eventually director of the U.S. National Security Agency (NSA). We are also deeply grateful for the assistance of certain French nongovernmental organizations (NGOs)—Medicine de Monde and Action Nord Sud— and to Michelle, Pascal, Elizabeth, Claire, and others.

I also wish to thank the numerous Kurds who sheltered and fed us during our time in Turkey, and the several Turkish military officers who allowed us to stay, when they could easily have followed orders and returned us to Iraq. We will never forget the Turkish police officer and his wife, who sheltered my wife when the other family members were being detained. We are deeply grateful for all this assistance.

Ch. 01- The Kurds

My name is Taha Muhamad. I am a Kurd, now residing in Lonsdale, Minnesota, a small community approximately thirty miles south of the Twin Cities. My story, however, is rooted in Kurdish history; and it begins in Kirkuk, Iraq, a city and a region with a rich and tangled history.

Who are the Kurds?
The Kurds are people with their own language and culture. Approximately 40 million Kurds live in a mountainous region of southwest Asia, in an area that straddles the borders of Turkey, Iraq, Iran, Armenia, and Syria. About 15 million Kurds reside in southeastern Turkey. They are a non-Arabic people who speak a language related to Persian.

The 1920 Treaty of Sevres, which created the modern states of Iraq, Syria, and Kuwait, was to have included the possibility of a Kurdish state, but that promise was never kept. Following the overthrow of the Turkish monarchy by Kemal Ataturk, the countries of Turkey, Iran, and Iraq all agreed that they would not recognize an independent Kurdish state.

The Kurds in Turkey
The Turkish government under Ataturk treated the Kurds in an especially harsh manner, designating them "Mountain Turks," outlawing their language, and forbidding them to wear traditional Kurdish costumes in the cities. The government also encouraged migration of Kurds to the cities; a measure intended to reduce the

upland population. The Turkish government still does not recognize Turkish Kurds as a minority group within the Turkish population.

Turkish forces put down Kurdish uprisings in the 1920s and 1930s, but then the Kurdish struggle lay dormant for several decades. In 1978, Abdullah Ocalan, one of seven children from a poor farming family, established the Kurdish Workers' Party, or PKK, a political organization and movement that advocated independence. In 1979, Ocalan fled Turkey, relocating in Syria. In 1984, Ocalan's PKK began an armed struggle, recruiting thousands of young Kurds who were driven by poverty and by Turkish repression of their language and culture.

Turkish forces fought the PKK guerrillas for years; a costly conflict that took an estimated 30,000 Kurdish lives. Ocalan had been directing his guerrillas from Syria, but in 1998 Damascus (under pressure from Ankara) expelled him, and he began a multi-nation odyssey, until finally being captured in Nairobi on January 15, 1999, and taken to Turkey, where a death sentence was turned into a life sentence.

The Kurds in Iran

In 1946, Kurds, with Soviet backing, succeeded in establishing the republic of Mahabad, but a year later the Iranian monarch crushed the embryonic state. In 1979, the turmoil surrounding Iran's revolution allowed the Kurds to establish an unofficial border area, free of Iranian government control. Kurds, however, were unable to hold the area for long.

The Kurds in Iraq

The Iraqi Kurds have over the years also faced severe repression. Kurds in northern Iraq, under a British mandate, staged revolts in 1919, 1923, and 1932—but were crushed each time. Under Mustafa Barzani, they continued to wage an intermittent struggle against Baghdad. In 1970, Baghdad granted Kurds language rights and self rule, but the deal broke down partly over oil revenues. In 1974, new clashes erupted, and Iraq forced 130,000 Kurds into Iran. Iran, however, withdrew support for the Kurds the following year.

Kurds were in fight with Iraqi Government in the 1980-88 Iran-Iraq war. Saddam Hussein, after ceasefire signed between Iraq and Iran, brutally retaliated, razing villages and attacking Kurdish populations with chemical weapons, killing 5,000 Kurds in the town of Halabja. The Kurds rebelled again following the Persian Gulf War, only to be crushed again by Iraqi troops. About two million fled to Iran; five million currently remain in Iraq. Following the Gulf war, The United States tried to create a safe haven for the Iraqi Kurds by imposing a "no-fly" zone north of the 36th parallel. In 1991, northern Iraq's Kurdish area came under international protection.

Current status

Despite a common goal of independent statehood, the 40 million or so of Kurds in the various countries are hardly unified. From 1994 to 1998, two Iraqi Kurdish factions—the Kurdistan Democratic Party, led by Massoud Barzani, and the Patriotic Union of Kurdistan, led by Jalal Talabani—waged a bloody war

17

for control of northern Iraq. In September of 1998, the two sides agreed to a power-sharing arrangement.

In 2003, the Americans deposed Hussein, the Kurds' most hated enemy, and opening the way for Kurds to establish control over their mountainous, Switzerland-size territory. Though they remained part of Iraq, they established an autonomous region. Among Kurdish groups, those in Iraq are closest to realizing independence. They have a parliament and a president, oil pipelines of their own, and a military force called the peshmerga, which roughly means "those who face death."

Remaining part of Iraq has long seemed a necessary evil—more a condition demanded by the West, and specifically by the Americans, than a Kurdish desire. Since the fall of Saddam Hussein, the Kurdish government has hinted that it might secede from Iraq—a message that enrages its powerful neighbors, Turkey and Iran, as well as Iraqi Arabs in the south.

Since 2003, investment, development, and oil-fueled optimism (Kurdistan sits atop vast oil deposits) has transformed the region. Some five million Kurds entered into what many called a golden decade—an era free of fear. In the year 2016, this era of stability is now under threat, as the Islamic State (ISIS) continues its threats.

Note

This historical overview is intended to provide only the briefest introduction to a complex twentieth-century history. Those interested in gaining a greater understanding of the rich and tortured Kurdish history will benefit from the following sources:

Kurdistan: In the Shadow of History
Susan Meiselas and Martin van Bruinessen
A History of the Kurdish People
Hamma Mirwaisi
The Miracle of the Kurds: A Remarkable Story of Hope Reborn in Northern Iraq
Stephen Mansfield
The Kurds in Iraq: The Past, Present and Future
Kerim Yildiz
A Modern History of the Kurds
David McDowall
Invisible Nation: How the Kurds Quest for Statehood is Shaping Iraq and the Middle East.
Quil Lawrence

Ch. 02- Parents and Grandparents

Grandfather Muhammad, Sr., and Grandmother Basty

On an ordinary day in 1896, my grandfather Muhammad, Sr. and his friend, Nazim, were mischievously shooting their rifles into the air, while racing their horses outside their village, Panja Ali, a small community near the oil rich city of Kirkuk. A stray bullet from Nazim's rifle pierced Muhammad's back. He fell off his horse and lay on the ground, motionless and unconscious.

Nazim rushed to his aid, all the while shouting for help. Several clan members, hearing the cries, arrived at the scene. Muhammad, Sr., barely conscious, stated clearly that the incident had not been a malicious act, and that Nazim was not to be harmed. Shortly after uttered these words, my grandfather passed away.

Following the funeral, the family informed Nazim that they would honor Muhammad's wish and that he would not be harmed. He was, however, asked to leave the village in order to avoid any future tensions. Nazim agreed, and he moved to an undisclosed location. On the day my grandfather died, his youngest son was three months old: his name was Ameen. My grandmother, Basty, changed the infant's name to Muhammad, Jr., to honor her late husband. Muhammad, Jr. is my father.

Her unrelenting grief over the loss of her husband caused my grandmother to lose her vision. So, Muhammad, Jr. grew up without a father and in the care of a sightless mother. Nonetheless, Muhammad, Jr. and his older brother, Ali, eventually became responsible adults. The family tragedy compelled my father, Muhammad, Jr., to work hard at his farming tasks, and he also became known as a villager who could treat gunshot wounds.

Safarberlik

With the advent of World War I, Russia declared war on the Ottoman Empire. The Turks responded by drafting men between the ages 16 and 60 from Arab and Kurdish areas—and forcing them to fight with Turkish (Ottoman) soldiers against the Russians. When Ottoman regional and local officials declared the beginning of a conscription process in a locale, they began their loud announcements with the word Safarberlik. Once Safarberlik was announced, conscription began, and young men were called, collected, and sent to the war front.

In 1914, Muhammad, Jr., my father, and other men living in Ottoman controlled territories were drafted to serve in the Ottoman ranks. They were sent to the Russian border, to help gain territory and further the aims of the Ottoman Empire. My father, who was nineteen at the time, was deployed close to the front lines, and when he arrived, he felt neither compelled nor willing to fight. In his view, it wasn't his war to fight, and he didn't feel obligated to fight with the Ottoman

Turks. He was after all a Kurd, and he had good reason to feel that way.

The Ottoman Turks had exploited Muslims and non-Muslims alike, and had taken Constantinople from Greece on May 6, 1453. They named the city "Islambul", which means "Revenue of Islam." After a few years, they changed the name to Istanbul, which in Turkish means "You get what you need." That city became a home only for Turks, not for Muslim Arabs or Kurds—and not for Christians or Jews.

All this history was passing through Muhammad, Jr.'s mind as he arrived with the Ottoman troops, to fight the Russians. He quickly decided that he must return to Kirkuk, to care for his blind mother and attend to the affairs of his family. He made his way back to his city, using various methods, including celestial navigation and night travel, to avoid detection.

He faced difficult challenges along the way. He had to avoid Ottoman soldiers, a constant danger, and he was forced to fight off two bandits. He crossed a number of rivers, while avoiding a snake bite and surviving on little food. He had with him, however, two loaded rifles, a pistol, and a dagger; and he was determined to make it home—to reunite with his mother.

He finally arrived in Kirkuk, dismounted from his horse, and kissed the ground. He was greatly relieved to have made it, relieved that he could now watch over his family, even though his older brother, Ali, was still away, fighting an ongoing war.

My maternal grandfather Muhammad Ibrahim Agha

During the course of WW I, the Ottoman military forces were unable to maintain control of Arab areas in Iraq, since the British Army had taken control. When the British army arrived on the outskirts of Kirkuk, my maternal grandfather (Muhammad Ibrahim Agha) felt crushed—he realized that the Ottoman Turks had retreated from Kirkuk.

My grandfather had served as a chaplain in the Ottoman army, and he was so heart-broken that he refused to return to his work. He believed that the Ottoman Turks were defenders of the Islam, and he refused to be a part of the new Iraqi government. He would not accept English money, stating and preaching that "earning a living from the English-Iraq is a sin." By the time he died, he had spent all of his savings and sold off most of his possessions in order to survive. He was willing to starve before working for a government that he considered to be disloyal to the Ottomans. I regret that my grandfather developed such a blind loyalty to a Kurdish enemy—the Ottoman Empire."

My Uncle Ali Basty and women at the public bathhouse

This story has been documented by a number of historians and writers. On May 4, 1924, in the city of Kirkuk, on the eve of Eid al-Fitr (the feast that marks the end of Ramadan), my Uncle Ali, my dad's older brother, had ridden his horse into the Imam Qasim neighborhood

23

near the Na'ib Oghlu mosque. This mosque stood across the street from a public bathhouse for women, known as Joot Hamam.

He sensed that something wasn't right, and then he spotted a uniformed column of armed British mercenaries making their way toward Joot Hamam. Hearing their gunfire, citizens ran for cover. Ali, recognizing that these men were up to no good, dismounted his horse, ran across the street, and climbed to the roof of a building. He got into a prone position, aimed his rifle at the approaching column, and began firing—hoping to drive them back. The mercenaries returned fire, and a gun battle ensued. An Arab visitor, who happened to be in the neighborhood, a man by the name of Hajji Rasheed, came to my uncle's aid. He too started firing in the direction of the British thugs. Both men, fighting to defend the honor of the town, but unfortunately, in the course of the gun battle; Hajji Rasheed was hit in the chest and instantly killed.

Ali kept firing until all the women had safely fled the bathhouse. The battle finally ended with more than twenty British mercenaries lying dead—and the rest in retreat. Ali—a tall, strong, blue-eyed hardened fighter, and a veteran of World War I action—had fought them off, and had saved the honor of many women. He became a hero, revered for his valor and gallantry.

Soon after the battle, the governor of Kirkuk received a telegram from Baghdad (from King Faisal I of Iraq) ordering the governor to arrest Ali and hang him on the banks of the Khasa River in Kirkuk. The governor, Majeed Al-Yakubi, sent a member of his security detail to warn Ali and my father of the danger and to tell them to leave Kirkuk immediately, to avoid execution. Majeed Al-Yakubi greatly appreciated Ali's defense of the women, and he was not about to allow his arrest and execution.

Ali and my dad left Kirkuk and joined Sheik Mahmoud's campaign, an effort to keep the English out of Kurdistan and a conflict that continued for a number of years. When the leader, Sheik Mahmoud, met Ali, he dismounted his horse and embraced him and thanked him for protecting the Kirkuk women. Ali and my dad fought alongside Mahmoud for six years, and years later the two brothers returned to Kirkuk.

Ch. 03- Father-In-law and Mother-In-Law

Khalid Agha (my father-In-law)

Khalid Agha was my father-In-law, the son of Salih Agha, an officer in the Ottoman Army. His mother was Layla Khan. Khalid Agha was born in Kirkuk, in 1919. Following graduation from high school, he entered a military aviation school in Baghdad.

Rasheed Ali al-Gailani was a revolutionary leader at the time, and his supporters, including Khalid, my father-in-law, opposed the British rule in Iraq. In April 1941, al-Gailani and the pro-Axis military group seized power and ejected Prince Emir Abdul Ilah bin Ali al-Hashimi, the pro-British regent for the child king, Faisal the Second. On May 1941, al-Gailani, with some German and Italian support, began fighting the regime.

By June 1941, those forces had been completely defeated, and Emir Abdul-Ilah was recalled. Rasheed Ali Al-Gailani escaped to Lebanon with four other officers. Three hundred of his men, including Khalid, were captured and jailed. Khalid was sentenced to a three-year prison term, and the court ordered that the other three hundred be hanged. On the day before the scheduled hanging, the court allowed family members of the condemned to visit, and to see their loved ones for the last time.

The prisoners, however, had secretly told their families to bring small tools—screwdrivers, hammers, and metal saws. The family members hid them in the foodstuffs   they had brought along, and as night covered the city of Baghdad, the prisoners, including Khalid, used the tools to break out the prison. Khalid headed toward Kirkuk, 250 miles away, with seven of his friends.

Khalid Agha and his family in Kirkuk

Khalid arrived safely, but his family members encouraged him to leave, fearing for his life and also fearing that the Iraqi government might punish them, for hiding him. They urged Khalid to go to Chemchamal, a village north of Kirkuk, where they thought he could safely reside for a time. Khalid took their advice, and he and a friend departed for the village, about an hour's drive north of Kirkuk. Upon arriving, Khalid decided to have lunch at a restaurant, and he remained there for three hours—he had heard that the police were looking for him.

As he contemplated his next move, Khalid noticed that the restaurant owner was talking to a couple of security officials, and he immediately sensed that they might be looking for him. The officials took a table and ordered some food, making it appear that they were just there to dine—and had no interest in Khalid.

Khalid asked the restaurant owner to watch his jacket while he visited the men's room. Once there, he and his friend escaped through the bathroom window and ran down the street, fearing for their lives. Khalid began asking people where he could find Kokha Afandi, who resided in the small town of Gazalan, about an hour's drive west of Chemchamal. Kokha Afandi was a close relative of Layla, Khalid's mother. Khalid finally met an individual who knew Kokha, and who agreed to take Khalid and his friend to Gazalan.

The two arrived at Kokha's residence, and were greeted by a young girl—Talatt, Kokha Afandi's daughter. In broken Kurdish, Khalid said, "I am looking for Kokha Afandi." Talatt at first thought that Khalid was a foreigner (perhaps an Englishman), since he did not speak Kurdish well and did not resemble the Kurdish villagers. Khalid was indeed Kurdish, but he did not speak the language. He spoke only Turkish, a consequence of the Ottoman Empire influence.

Talatt then ran off to tell her mother, Peroz, that two young men were looking for her father, Kokha Afandi. Peroz came to the door and welcomed the visitors, and told a male helper to open the large visitor hall, where Khalid and his friend were served coffee and tea. Other men immediately butchered a young lamb, and Peroz ordered her helpers to prepare some rice and Kurdish breads. News of the visitors reached other villagers, and the Gazalan men visited and warmly greeted Khalid Agha and his Kirkuk friend. Children, young men, and young girls assembled outside the visitors' hall, while the men went off to find Kokha Afandi and inform him of the visitors.

Khalid Agha and Kokha Afandi
The men located Kokha Afandi and ten of his men, who were about to mount their horses and head to

another village, to resolve some tribal problems related to a bloody fight that had occurred forty days earlier. When he got news of the visitors, however, he canceled his trip, and sent one of his men to inform villagers that he could not meet with them on this day.

When Kokha Afandi arrived at his home, he went immediately to the visitors' hall, where Khalid Agha was awaiting him. Khalid hugged him, but Kokha Afandi had no idea who he was, whereupon Khalid introduced himself, saying, "My father is Salih Agha Qamchee Rash." The two then went to the main part of the house, where Afandi said to Peroz, his wife, "Do you know who is here?" "No," she said, "I don't know." Afandi said, "This is Khalid, my cousin, Layla Khan's son! He is Prince!"

After a huge dinner, the two men stayed up late conversing, and Khalid told Kokha Afandi about his escape from the Baghdad jail, and his trip to Kirkuk, and then his trip to Gazalan. Kokha Afandi then told him that he could stay at the house as long as he wished.

Two days later government officials learned of Khalid's whereabouts, and security and police officials came to Gazalan looking for him. Afandi then sent him, together with three horsemen, to another village, to hide. Khalid's friend, however, was unable to cope with the rugged mountainous environment, and he sent word to his family members that he needed help in getting to Kirkuk. The mayor of Chemchamal continued his efforts to find and arrest Khalid, but Kokha Afandi responded by moving him around to various villages, hiding him and thwarting the officials.

Kokha Nasih Gazalani (Kokha Afandi's Grandson)

Three weeks later a large number of Iraqi soldiers showed up at Kokha Afandi's residence, at night, looking for Khalid, who was indeed at the house. Kokha put Khalid in a room where his wife, sisters, and daughters spent time. The women proceeded to put on an act. They put Khalid into a dress, and placed him under a blanket, and told the soldiers that he was a daughter-in-law who was in labor and about to deliver a baby. Out of respect, the military people did not enter the room, Khalid was again saved; but for the next seven years, he would be forced to hide in one house or another, or in one cave or another.

Khalid and Talatt's wedding

Seven years passed, and Talatt turned fourteen, whereupon her father, Kokha Afandi, allowed a religious marriage agreement to be written for Talatt and Khalid. Khalid then moved (alone) to another village called Dalow, He bought some land and established a farm, a venture that eventually employed about eight farm workers.

Several weeks after arriving at Dalow, the marriage was ready to be consummated, and a horses' convoy was organized to escort Talatt from Gazalan to Dalow. The bride's mother, however, opposed the marriage, and she tried to block the convoy; but Kokha Afandi intervened, and allowed the convoy to proceed. As it neared the village of Dalow, convoy members began shooting their rifles into the air, a way of celebrating the upcoming marriage. Talatt, however, had begun to weep, as had her mother and both wept all the way to Dalow.

After a year of marriage, Khalid and Talatt produced a baby girl. Khalid's joy, however, was tempered by the knowledge that his Kirkuk friend had been hanged, on orders from the Iraqi governor in Kirkuk. His friend had turned himself in, believing the King's word—believing that the escapees from the Baghdad jail would be forgiven. It was a ruse. The King never intended to provide any forgiveness.

31

Talatt Khan and thieves

Khalid continued to evade authorities, and one day he decided to visit relatives in the nearby village of Gazalan. He had taught Talatt how to use a gun, fearing for her safety when left alone, and thieves had somehow learned that she would be alone. They decided to steal some of Khalid's horses that night, but the farm dogs spotted their presence, and the barking awakened Talatt, who saw the thieves trying to enter the horse barn. Talatt grabbed the gun and began firing over their heads, a sound that awakened the farm guards. The thieves fled, and the guards began to pursue them, but Talatt called them back. She did not want to see a life destroyed over an attempted horse theft.

All this commotion awakened the villagers, who assembled at Talatt's home, carrying guns and vowing to support this young woman who had displayed so much courage and boldness. Khalid returned the next day and was told of the event. The news also reached residents of other villages, and they too eventually came to admire Talatt's courage.

Young villager Kareem Shafa

One day, Khalid instructed Kareem Shafa, one of his farm workers, to deliver a message and a sum of money to a shop in Kirkuk, and to purchase a certain item noted in the message. The young man, Kareem, could not read, but was told that the note contained the name of a headache medicine, which he was to purchase. So, on a summer morning, before daybreak, Kareem jumped on his donkey and hit the dusty trail that took him over hills and farm lands to Kirkuk—a journey of three hours or more by donkey.

So, Kareem arrived in Kirkuk and started asking for the location of the shop, which he eventually found. He tied his donkey to a lamppost, entered the shop, and handed over the note. He saw the shop owner began to smile, but he did not ask why the owner seemed amused. The owner gave Kareem a bottle filled with liquid, wrapped in brown paper and sealed. The owner said to Kareem, "Do not open this on the way home, and do not show it to others."

Kareem left the shop, but then noticed that his donkey, which had been tied to a lamppost, was missing. This surprised him, but then he spotted some boys playing a game with the donkey. One would try to ride, and others would try to push him off, to allow another to mount the beast. Kareem angrily ordered the boys to return the donkey, but the boys ignored him. Kareem placed the wrapped bottle on the ground and proceeded to reclaim his donkey. A fight then ensued between Kareem and the boys, and Kareem used a stick to crack a few heads, a tactic that sent the boys running.

His shouts had caught the attention of the shop owner, who came out and quickly spotted the wrapped bottle, lying on the ground. The owner picked up the bottle, to keep it safe, and when Kareem finally rescued his donkey, the owner handed it over to him. Kareem then mounted his donkey and, feeling relieved, rode out of town. But what did the bottle contain?

Weeks passed, and one day Kareem got hit with a severe headache. Khalid had hidden the bottle in a stream near a field, to keep it cool. Kareem knew the whereabouts of the bottle and decided that its contents would relieve his headache. He located the bottle and pulled it from the waterwheel, and began sipping on the mysterious liquid, as though he were drinking pure water or perhaps fruit juice. But he was in for a surprise.

The contents of the bottle apparently contained a strong drug, one that caused Kareem to begin engaging in some strange behaviors. He would jump into the air, as though stung by a snake, then fall heavily to the ground. He would regain his feet and then began spinning like a Turkish and Syrian Muslim Dervish. He would then suddenly jump into the stream and began swimming, as though pursuing his lover. He kept making strange movements and singing strange songs, behavior that attracted villagers, who noticed the empty bottle in his hand.

The villagers then located Khalid and informed him of Kareem's behavior, telling him that he had lost his mind and had become became the village's first crazy person. Khalid arrived at the scene and quickly spotted the empty bottle. He began laughing, and the villagers thought for a moment that Khalid had also lost his mind.

Khalid picked up Kareem Shafa and began dipping him into the stream, further confusing the villagers. Khalid continued the dipping process until Kareem regained his senses, but he did not reveal the contents of the bottle. In fact, it contained wine, a drink that the Islamic religion forbids. Everything eventually returned to normal, and everyone returned to their normal activities.

Khalid Agha and the navigation job

In 1951, the government pardoned those who had escaped from the prison, but Khalid decided to stay in Dalow for a time. He was enjoying the rural life, but in time he got hit by a mysterious disease, one similar to malaria, and he was bedridden for two weeks. Talatt, fearing for his life, instructed Kareem to travel to Kirkuk and inform Khalid's brothers and sisters that he was seriously ill. The family members immediately traveled to Dalow village and took Khalid to Kirkuk, where he recovered.

He returned to the village, but then decided to move the entire family to Kirkuk. He turned his land and livestock over to the villagers, and gave Kokha Afandi some land, in appreciation for having saved his life seven years previous. Khalid was an experienced navigator, and he found employment at the airport in Ein-zala, in Kurdistan, where he worked for the British-Iraq Petroleum Company from 1951 to 1966.

Khalid raised pigeons (a hobby), and he was a very sociable individual. His house was always open to visitors, especially for the people of Gazalan, who had saved his life. He gave them land and helped them in many ways, always grateful for their hospitality and generosity and help.

Many people came to my father-in-law's house (Khalid Agha). Even though he did not personally know many of them, he would never ask them where they were from or why they were visiting him. He would feed them and allow them to stay as long as they wished. He would even give some of them cash gifts. He did this first for God—and for another reason. He always remembered that he, too, was once in that impoverished situation, a visitor in a strange land. The Kurdish people had respected him, fed him, clothed him—and even let him wed one of their own. He never forgot.

Ch. 04- Earliest Years: Some Recollections

Bear encounter

In the year 1925, my father, Muhammad, Jr., and his brother, Ali, left Kirkuk to join Sheikh Mahmoud Barzanji in a series of Kurdish uprisings against the British Mandate in Iraq. Attempts to establish an independent Kurdistan, however, ultimately failed, and my father returned to Kirkuk in 1937, at which time he married my mother, Sabriah.

My father told me about an incident that occurred in my very early childhood. I was three years old, and we were taking a walk in the groves outside Kirkuk. A tall bear suddenly confronted us, and it seemed ready to attack. My brave father, however, quickly responded. He grabbed his dagger, the one with a red ivory handle, and waved it at the bear, back and forth and up and down. He thought he might have to attack the bear, perhaps go for its neck, but the beast finally retreated. All the while, I acted bravely, the way my father was acting, and together we repelled the bear.

As the bear continued to retreat, its owner, an Englishman, appeared. The bear belonged to him, and he asked my father to stop brandishing the dagger. He then ordered his bear to retreat. The Englishman happened to be a petrol engineer, working in the oil fields around Kirkuk. (At the time, eighty percent of revenues went to the English; twenty percent went to the Iraqi government.) The Englishman had been impressed by my father's courage, and he apologized for having

37

frightened us. He then asked if my father would go to work for him at the Iraqi Petroleum Company, serving as a bodyguard.

We returned home, and my father related the bear story, a tale that circulated for many years among relatives and friends. My father accepted the Englishman's job offer and stayed employed with the Iraqi Petroleum Company for thirteen years, faithfully serving as a personal guard.

Insane Shakir, our neighbor

Our house sat in a long alley with a closed off end. One neighbor seemed especially frightening, a forty-year-old man named Shakir, who happened to be crazy. He was a carpenter by trade, and he possessed sharp tools that he used for wood cutting and furniture making. Our house sat directly across from his, where he lived with his mother and younger brother, and I was told to keep my distance, to avoid this crazed individual.

Shakir was very religious; and sometimes at night we could hear him calling out the name of God. My father was a humble man, and Shakir understood, and when he would lapse into an insane state, terrifying the neighbors, my father would go to him and shout, "Stop this violence, Shakir." Then my dad would hug the troubled man and calm him down, and Shakir would put his head on my father's shoulder--and cry and sweat. I was just a kid, and those scenes always scared me, but I always admired my father for the way he handled Shakir's madness.

Shakir's front yard, which was fenced off by a high muddy brick wall, contained a huge black mulberry tree. One could enter the yard through an old wooden door in the wall, and one summer day my young eyes saw that the door was open, allowing me to spot the mulberries scattered around beneath the tree. I went home and got a ceramic bowl and returned to collect some black mulberries. Although I knew it was a potentially dangerous venture, I quietly made my way into the yard, and then saw Shakir, who was sitting under the tree and striking a piece of wood with an ax. No one else was home; he was alone.

Fearful as I was, I began to pick up the delicious black berries, whereupon Shakir ceased his wood cutting, lifted his head, and looked at me with his wide scary eyes. I was determined to mask my fear and to conduct myself as I knew that my father would conduct himself. I told myself that I had no reason to fear Shakir, and I continued to collect the berries. I filled the ceramic bowl and left without saying a word--no thank you and no goodbye.

I was a kid, and still didn't even know how to say thank you or goodbye—I didn't know those words. I was like a little bird, picking up small sesame seeds from under the feet of a hungry cat. If it is a truism that God saves little kids, maybe guardian angels were watching over me. Shakir could have cut me into small pieces and thrown the bits to the little birds that gathered around the mulberry tree.

As an adult, looking back, I still feel a chill when I recall the way Shakir attacked his widowed mother, Gulostan, with an ax. I can still hear her screams. Neighbors also heard them and locked their doors. I stood with my mother inside our house, peering toward Shakir's dwelling. I was so scared that I soiled myself. I heard mother Gulostan continue to scream—and then silence. She had become a corpse.

The neighbors, the creek people, stayed in their rooms, awaiting my father's return from his humble shop. When he finally arrived, they related the event, and then the police arrived. My father helped them apprehend Shakir, who was sent to Baghdad, where the mental health doctors decided he should be put to death by lethal injection. From that terrible day forward, I never again tried to collect mulberries from Shakir's yard. And for many years, the image of his crazed eyes and the sound of his deadly assault on his mother stayed with me—day and night, awake or asleep.

Taha at school—my father's school
My father had been unable to attend school; the Ottoman officials would not allow Kurds to pursue an education. But my father served as a "school" for the entire family even was unable to read and write, telling stories about the Prophets and the heroes at Rustam Zal. He taught us to help others, to stand firmly with the right, and to reject falsehoods. He taught me how to conduct myself; and he shared his knowledge about the Islam religion, human rights, and various laws.

My mother, Sabriah, took care of the entire family--kids, elders, and visitors. She was generous, and she would often send hot breads to neighbors. She was also smart, brave, and strong. My father greatly respected her, and they shared happy times together. I learned from both. I learned kids' games and other activities, but I only participated in those games I thought were good and beneficial. I avoided the mischievous activities that my friends seemed to enjoy. I remember making little waterfalls. I would place small green tree branches on both banks of a small stream, pretending that it was a river connected to a large waterfall surrounded by huge trees.

I would also climb the tall black and white mulberry trees, and I would shake berries onto a sheet below that the neighbors held. I would frequently study my history books under those trees. I would make little houses with mud and rocks collected from the stream that passed by our house. I would also make small models of cars, using different types of wires. I would connect battery operated lamps to the cars and drive them in both daylight and (using the lamps) nighttime hours, imagining that I was navigating tough roads.

Night kite and colorful stars
I made and flew kites. I would hang various colored candles on the strings, and when lit they resembled colored stars. I often wondered why God did not make colored stars. I once made especially big candle lights for my kite, which I put up one summer

night. My brother and my neighbors and their kids watched the kite's flight from their rooftops, and some folks actually fell asleep on their roofs. The kite with its lighted candles eventually came down on a date tree, and we feared that the tree would catch fire. But the tree was green, and the candle flamed out—and I was saved from my dad's punishment.

I then decided that I had to create safer lights for my kites. So, I made electric lamplights, using long wires from a broken electric generator. But the wires and the lamps had poor connections, and they didn't last very long, since I didn't know how to effectively use welding equipment. I became proficient at kite making, and neighborhood kids would ask me to make kites for them. One summer holiday I made twenty kites and began selling them to the neighborhood kids. But I came to believe that is was shameful to profit in that way, to take money from other kids, so I stopped selling on the third day.

I would visit mosques to pray, and on Friday nights I would sometimes watch a ring of Dervishes strike themselves with daggers and hold blazing hot charcoals. I would attend Islamic celebrations, whenever someone came over from Hajj. Once, when I was ten, I joined a group of neighbors who were part of a procession moving toward a Kirkuk cemetery. I remember being part of a procession and holding a dead baby wrapped in white grave clothes (a coffin. I was afraid, but I knew I had to continue, and I tried to hide my fear. Finally, another group member volunteered to carry the dead child. For many nights, I had nightmares about this experience, but the people of our creek, our neighbors, praised me for my assistance.

I took instruction from my father, but I also listened to stories told by neighbors, especially those told by Uncle Sarkees, an Armenian; Uncle Saeed, a shoe-repairer; Uncle Shafeeq, a grocer; and Allah Weardy, a butcher.

I once decided to make a bicycle in the shape of a little car. I collected some rusted scrap metal and put it together, and my mother seemed to admire my inventiveness. But my father just laughed, and waited to see what I would do with that collection of scrap. I had few tools to work with—only a hammer, a wood saw, and some screwdrivers—and my plan ultimately failed. I finally reached school age, and my life began to change.

Ch. 05- Taha's School Registration: 1951

We all remember our first school experience. Mine was a bit unusual. My father, mother, sisters, and brothers were not formally educated, although one brother was receiving lessons from an elderly woman by the name of Mullah Hamdia. She was teaching him the holly book Quran, and he was in the final year with her.

One day, as I stood watching kids from our neighborhood preparing to register for elementary school. I asked, "How I can register my name at the school?" They said, "Bring your birth certificate and one adult with you." The school was called the Male Elementary Al-Mustansaria School, and its principal was Khalid Beck. He was elderly, and well-known for gazing at pretty women. He would put his hand over his eyebrows to shade his eyes, and then continue gazing and staring, up and down, back and forth, from head to toe.

After learning about school registration and the possibility of attending school, I ran home and said to my mother, "Give me my birth certificate. I am going to register my name at the school." She thought I was kidding, and said, "Go away from me, because I am so sick." I persisted, and I asked again, tears falling from my eyes, "Please, Mom, give me my birth card." This was a difficult demand for her. She had no permission to give me my birth card, since it was an important identification document. I repeated my demand, which angered her, and she began throwing shoes and wooden

44

slippers at me, trying to chase me way. But I would not quit.

She finally said to me, "Go ask your father first." I immediately took off on a run to my father's tiny clothing shop, approximately a mile away, and I arrived out of breath. My heart was beating fast, my mouth was dry, and my face was pale. My father was surprised to see me, but glad to see me, his youngest son. I kissed his hand, and he hugged me. One boy about my age was standing nearby, balancing a tray of small cakes on his head. My father bought me one, and I gave him an appreciative smile, but I thought to myself: "Why is this kid not telling his father to register him at the school?"

As I stood in the shop, eating the cake, my father asked, "Taha, why are you here?" I told him in a clear and brave voice, "I need my birth certificate because I need to register at the school!" He laughed and said, "Go home and ask your mom to give you the birth certificate. Watch out for speeding cars, horse wagons, bad boys, mad dogs, and insane people. And watch out for the nails on the street; they can stick into your bare feet."

I immediately took off for home, running all the way, faster than a deer. I was so happy. Every hair on my head was celebrating and dancing, as the dust rose up and hit me in the face. I don't know how many times I fell and scraped my knees, but I did not stop running. The prospect of school stirred my young heart, and I did not feel the pain.

45

I arrived home, again out of breath. My mom had been worried about me. She hugged me, and I kissed her hand and said, "Father told me that you should give me my birth certificate." She began searching for it, and after opening many boxes, she found it. She then cleaned my knees, washing away the blood and dust, but I felt no pain. I had my birth certificate!

My oldest brother's wife, Nazira, accompanied me to the school, after wrapping herself in a black cloak and covering herself. We stopped some distance from the school building to see if we could spot someone we knew. Kids surrounded us, waiting to see what we would do with the birth card. Finally, we saw a man named Ahmad Jalal, an athletic instructor. My brother's wife gave him my certificate, and he grabbed my hand, and together we marched to the school. Principal Khalid Beck registered me and said, "Come next week to begin attending." I was so happy. I said to myself, "Thank you God."

Kids were waiting for me as I left the school; and we all began singing, dancing, and clapping. I had registered at the school! I returned home, and saw that some neighbor women had come over to congratulate my mom for having enrolled me at a school. My oldest brother bought me new pants and shirts, some pencils and erasers, a pencil sharpener, and a green metal book box.

Al- Mustansaria Elementary School

On the first day, in September 1951, I walked to the school, holding my nice green metal book, which contained only a pencil, a pencil sharpener, and an eraser. All the students were standing in a line, in the front yard of the school. I was happy and nervous. The teachers, principal's assistant, and principal introduced themselves, and I noticed that each held a stick. They explained the rules of the school, and showed us the sticks, which they said would be used on students who broke the school rules. After the school officials had checked our names, we divided into classes.

Mr. Shawkat: my first grade teacher

At our first class, we met the teacher, Mr. Shawkat, a short, fat little man. He told us, "Each student must bring two notebooks for tomorrow." Next day, as I sat waiting for class to start, Mr. Shawkat began checking to make sure each student had two notebooks. I did not have them; I had not taken seriously the teacher's order. Others had also failed to bring the required notebooks, and when Mr. Shawkat came to them, he would begin beating them. As he approached me, I stood up like a lawyer and said, "I told my father to buy two notebooks, but he did not buy them for me."

Mr. Shawkat stared at me. I looked like a normal child, and I did not look confused. He then summoned the school worker, Shakir, and gave him ten fils of Iraqi money (one Iraqi dinar = 1000 fils) and said to him, "Go buy two notebooks." As quick as a magic lamp's genie, Shakir was gone. He returned with two notebooks, which Shawkat handed to me. I thanked him, but I felt ashamed. I had saved my small, thin hands from the pain of the stick, but now I wondered how I could save myself from the punishment of God, for having made my innocent father look guilty. I decided from that moment on to tell only the truth, and I told my parents what had happened, on this second day of school.

I was the first child in my family to attend school, and each day after school I would try to share my new found knowledge with my brother, Musa, who was one year older, and with my friend, Ramiz. I advised my father to quit smoking: Mr. Shawat had described the dangers. I did my homework at home, on a mat made of plants, since we had no tables and chairs, and at night I studied under the light of a smoky oil lamp, since our house had no electricity. I studied hard for a full year— and then learned at the end of the year that I had not passed first grade. I had performed well, and to this day I still don't know why I hadn't passed.

Still in grade one, in my second year at Al-Mustansaria Elementary School
In September 1952, my brother Musa and my friend Ramiz enrolled in second year, although I was repeating first grade. My youngest sister had asked my father and mother to register her in the female elementary school, but I was opposed to it. I thought that it was shameful for a girl to attend school. Our culture was tough, and in my later adult years, I felt so sorry for her. Many girls were not allowed to attend school, maybe because of misunderstandings about our culture and our religion. My sister is now the mother of seven

beautiful daughters, and all have earned college degrees. One of them is a medical doctor in Erbil, a city in Kurdistan. My sister encouraged all of them to gain an education and to pursue their dreams and goals.

I felt fortunate to be able to attend school. I paid attention to the teachers, and I studied my subjects. I would return home immediately each day after school, but then I would leave my house to play football with the other kids on our neighborhood. I still have vivid memories of those childhood days.

Unfortunately, in many schools the desks were in poor repair, seriously damaged. The light was poor, making it difficult for the thirty to forty students to read and follow along with the instruction. In winter, the broken windows let in the cold, and in summer the heat caused great discomfort.

Ch. 06- Second Grade—and Various Events

My Left Leg (1953)

It was March of 1953. I was in grade two. My father had to take my sick mother to Baghdad for a surgical operation, and I was so sad, because I knew the road between Kirkuk and Baghdad was dangerous. I knew that there were road thieves in the Baqoba province area, and I knew that winter floods often killed travelers on that road.

I returned from school one day and saw that my mother had left. I ran out of the house, and suddenly found myself on the ground. I had been hit by a fat man on a bicycle, and when I tried to stand up, I immediately fell back on the road. I felt a warm liquid on my leg, and then I was surrounded by neighbors. They told me that my left leg was broken, and each wanted to help me stand up. My brother, Ahmad Agha, however, took over and put me on a horse wagon.

I appreciated my brother's help, and I was happy to be on the horse wagon; and I started to recall all the times I had secretly hung on to the back of it. The wagon man would discover our presence, and he would hit us with his horse lash.

We arrived at the Qoria Police District, and then my oldest brother took me (on his bicycle) to the Kirkuk Hospital. A nurse wrapped my broken leg, a temporary measure, and I was allowed to stay in the hospital for one night. I was in pain, and I had a bad feeling about my mom. She was at a hospital in Baghdad, and I was in a hospital in Kirkuk. My uncle, Ali, visited me and gave me fifty fils. A relative named Ibraheem, who was in the police force visited me and gave me a candy. I didn't sleep the whole night, and I kept other patients awake with my crying. The next morning my oldest brother came to the hospital and carried me to the operating room. The nurse wrapped my leg in white cement, and then my brother took me home.

A month later, my mother and father returned from Baghdad. When my mom saw the wrapped leg, her color turned yellow, and she immediately contracted a fever sickness. She was very worried about me. My poor father took her to Sulaymaniyah to see a medical specialist, a visiting doctor from a foreign country. After only one week, however, my mom and I recovered. During the time I was disabled, my brother, M, brought me my school assignments.

Taha and flood—1954

On a March day in 1954, a huge black cloud covered the sky, and for a short time, it rained cats and dogs. Water filled the city of Kirkuk. Our innocent stream became a devil, sending waves of muddy water to our rooms. My books and notebooks were dancing on the waves, and I could not control them, and I was afraid that the water would continue to rise. So my brother, Ahmad, put me on his shoulder and took me to the neighbor's house, where we spent the night.

The next day we came back to our flooded house and cleaned it. I collected my school materials, and we all waited days for our blankets and herbal mats to dry. Our stream finally changed from devil to angel, and returned to normal. I have retained vivid recollections of that stream. I recall the colorful rocks and the times I played with the fish, frogs, and turtles. After the flood, Kirkuk city extended city water to our house, and we were able to stop getting our water from the stream.

Taha at the feast

Each year, my father would take me shopping, preparing for Ramadan Feast. He would buy me clothes, and shoes that were always one size too large, so that I could wear them for a full year, as I continued to grow. The soles would develop holes, but I wouldn't tell anyone. I didn't want to embarrass my father. He was poor, and I knew he was unable to buy a second pair. One pair had to last the entire year. I patched the holes with paper and even empty cigarette packages, anything to keep my feet dry in the winter season.

Ten days before the Feast, I was organizing kids in our neighborhood area, preparing them for the Feast days. One kid, Mahmoud, was blind, but we would include him. Our group spent the Feast day in the Kirkuk streets, taking part in various activities and visiting colorful places. We rode donkey wagons, visited ice-cream shops, and attended movies.

Kirkuk had many cinemas, with names like Ghazy, Hamraah, Alamein, Njoom, Atlas, and Khayam.

There were two types of cinema tickets: civilian and military. Civilian tickets cost 40 fils (1 Iraqi dinar =1000 fils), and military tickets cost 20 fils. We paid soldiers twenty fils to buy tickets for us. The cinema gate man would let us in with those military tickets, but I don't know why. Maybe because of we were kids.

Once inside, we would take seats nearest the screen and close to the egg sandwich sellers. We didn't seem to care about the millions of flies hovering above the sandwiches. We were interested in those unhealthy foods, and we tended to ignore the good food at home. We would occupy many more seats than we needed, and although we didn't wish to get into fights with bad kids, having that many seats under our control would sometimes lead to fights.

We had toy handguns and paper bullets, and when we fired them they would make a loud popping sound and emit smoke. Some kids would hold balloons and blow their whistles. The oldest boys, none from our group, would smoke and pollute the air. We all carried lots of sunflower seeds in our pockets, except for Mahmoud, the blind boy, who often brought with him a big can of sunflower seeds and dry garbanzos, a delicacy that had been heated in hot sand over a fire.

Sometimes we would watch a Tarzan movie, and when Tarzan killed a lion, we would start clapping. My blind friend, Mahmoud, would ask me what had happened, and I would tell him. Mahmoud would then put his seed can on the floor and also begin clapping. I was always glad that I could bring some happiness to my blind friend, on the day of the Feast. His mom trusted me to take care of him on all those days. I attended the cinema only during Feast times, and during those times I would dream about coming to America. But how and when? There were no answers to my questions--money, language, and age issues all stood in the way.

We kids would also visit swing sites, and at the city fair we would watch the Kurd magician, Hameed Chik-Chikanee, get someone to lay an egg. We also applauded the acrobats, and we would stay until we had spent all our money, and then return home, hungry and thirsty. Some children engaged in fights, and some came away with broken heads and ruined clothes.

Turkmen Shiite and hareesa soup

On Ashora day, we would visit the nearby village of Tsin, whose people were Turkmen Shiite. Ashora day commemorated the memory of the martyrs Hussein and Hassan, who were sons of Imam Ali and grandsons of the prophet Muhammad. We would arrive early in the morning and share in the sadness of that day. Tsin's people prepared food for visitors, including a dish called harisa, which was a thick soup full of nuts and raisins. Tsin villagers opened their houses and invited people in, and served them harisa and fruits, juice and tea. At day's end, we would return to Kirkuk and talk for hours about what we had seen, heard, and tasted.

In Kirkuk, there was a famous Arab Shiite by the name of Austa Hoobi. He had come to Kirkuk from

Baghdad (south of Kirkuk) and had established a few companies. He had bus service contracts with the English-owned Iraqi Petroleum Company (IPC), and he transported Kirkuk workers from the city to the oil field. He also owned brick and carpentry factories, which provided bricks, doors, and wood window frames to the IPC. My oldest brother worked for him at the carpentry company. Mr. Hoobi was very rich, and each year he would make lots of hareesa on the day of Ashora, and he would make the hareesa available in many locations for those who were commemorating the event.

Hadidi Arabs and buffalo cheese cream

About twenty-five Arab Hadidi families resided in Kirkuk; they had come from Syria years earlier. They were very respectful people and known for raising buffalo. They were also known for their white cream (cheese cream, or in Iraqi dialect "geamer") and white butter. Their buffalos could be seen standing in a pond that collected rainwater, at a spot called Arasah. Their houses were located between Kirkuk high school and the Hussayniyah mosque, and some of the Hadidi families would sell their their expensive but tasty geamer in the Qouria Bazaar.

After harvest and Arab farmers

At the middle of each summer, our creek would host a group of visitors—friends and relatives of the Arab farmers' families. These visitors would ride their donkeys up from the agricultural area around Jabal Hamreen, bringing with them their tents, oil lanterns, rugs, blankets, dry food, and bread. They would pitch their tents on the dusty open big yard (Waqif Oko) in front of Mustansaria School, in Kirkuk, and they would stay about a week. They sold their agriculture products—hay, wheat, and barley—and also lamb, sheep, and goat manure; as well as eggs and wild birds. They lived quite a distance from Kirkuk, so they did not bring vegetables or fruits.

As kids, we enjoyed their visits, and we always looked forward to them each summer. We would ride their donkeys, but without their permission. The donkeys would often buck us off, and the owner would rescue the donkey, which he needed deliver his goods. But it was fun, and we would imagine we were riding horses in Texas.

We would ski on the hay and the dry manure, pretending that we were skiing down the slopes of an American mountain. There was a big difference, however, between us and Disneyland kids. We would be covered with hay and dry excrement dust. The children of Disneyland were covered with the sweet smell of roses. Nonetheless, we were happy kids, just as happy as the Disneyland kids.

We would always buy some of the farmers' products, and my father always treated them in a friendly fashion. We would pray together, and serve them water and various foods. They were like relatives, and I still remember the way we rode their donkeys.

Before and after harvest—and Kurdish farmers

At peak harvest season, a Kurdish farmer would load his donkey with one type of vegetable or fruit— cucumbers, melons, round water melons. One special vegetable was called tar-ouzy kahee (a cucumber type). It was about one-meter long, one-inch thick and hollow. It also came in a smaller size, one that resembled a regular cucumber. Some kids would sell one big tarauzy one day, or sell two by cutting one of them into rings and sprinkling salt on them. Sometimes farmers would load their donkey with one type of fruit, figs perhaps or grapes. The farms were on the outskirts of Kirkuk, and there was no need for the entire family to come into the city, to sell their products.

But after the harvest, the Kurdish farmers would come in, leading their donkeys, loaded with wheat, which they would sell in the alleyways. We would ride the donkeys in the alleys. Sometimes the farmers (two or more) would transport the wheat by hand, delivering it to the buyers' homes--a 100 kg (around 200 lbs.) bag.

Hanna Gawir and stray (bulk) dogs
In the spring, the Iraqi minister of health would order the director of the Kirkuk municipality to kill stray dogs. A hunter by the name of Hanna Gawir—a Christian man who could eat pork—would be hired by the English staff at the Kirkuk oil company (IPC) to hunt pigs for them. He used a rifle that belonged to his father, a weapon his dad had used when serving as a mercenary in the English army.

So, we would rejoice each year when beloved uncle Hanna Gawir would appear with his gun, with bands of bullets strapped to his chest. We would gather around him, expressing our concern about the dogs that he was about to kill. We feared the sound of the gun and the smoke that came out of the barrel. Nonetheless, we would watch as our brother, Hanna Gawir, aimed at a dog and then slowly pulled the trigger. The dog would hit the ground, spilling blood, and his soul would leave his body. Other dogs, the ones belonging to English women, would be spared.

The sight of these shootings would sometimes bring tears to my eyes, but I could not stop our beloved Hanna Gawir from completing his mission. The cleaning agent (the municipal sweeper) would load the dead dogs onto his donkey and take them to the Kirkuk outskirts, where he would burn them. One day I asked hunter Hanna Gawir, "Why do you kill these dogs?" He replied, "These dogs are a danger to society; their bites can infect people and make them crazy."

I would soon learn that Iraqis were killing one another in streets and alleys--the way Hanna Gawir killed stray dogs.

Ch. 07- Turkmen Hatred of Kurds

Conflict between Kurds and Turkmen, 1958

The golden period passed, and the tragic period set in, a period of conflict between Kurds and Turkmen in Kirkuk. Several months after the revolution of Abdulkareem Qasim, the political hunters turned the Turkmen against their fellow Kurds in Kirkuk, bringing grief to the hearts of both the Turkmen and the Kurds. The hunters were the following:

1) The Prime Minister of Iraq, Abdulkareem Qasim, annulled the Baghdad Pact, and so the West, led by the British, found an opportunity to overthrow Qasim, creating chaos.

2) Abdulkareem Qasim refused to join with Egypt and Syria, so the President of Egypt, Abdul Nasser, used Abdulsalaam Arif as a tool to bring down Qasim.

3) Syria turned the Ba'ath Party in Iraq against the Iraqi regime; because of Iraq's refusal to join the Arab unity cause.

4) Abdulkareem Qasim said, "The Arabs and Kurds are partners in this country." So Turkey incited Turkmen to turn against the Kurds in Kirkuk, in order to deprive Iraqi Kurds of their rights and to silence the Kurds in Turkey.

5) Ba'athists and Arab nationalists turned Kirkuk Turkmen against the Kurds in order to control Kirkuk after the fall of Abdulkareem Qasim.

The conspiracy against Abdulkareem Qasim was severe, and it turned the people of Kirkuk into scapegoats. This pain started on July 14, 1958. On this day, army Colonel Qasim led a revolt against King Faisal the Second, a rebellion that became chaotic. The Qasim followers killed the innocent King Faisal the Second, although they were supposed to take him to Saudi Arabia and to safety. The King's grandfather was from Saudi Arabia, and the English had made him king of Iraq, after pushing the Turks away from Arabic areas. Major Abdulsalaam Arif was a member of this revolutionary group.

I remember Abdulsalaam Arif coming to a Kirkuk military football field after the July 14, 1958, events and delivering a speech in which he said, "Arabs and Kurds are partners in Iraq." This statement from Iraqi leaders was untrue, since all Iraqis were partners in Iraq, not just the Arabs and Kurds. Turkmen did not blame Arabs for this partnership; they blamed only Kurds. I saw how Turkmen acted after Arif's speech. I was there, and I saw how the Turkmen political hunters were taking orders from top political wolves in and out of Iraq.

Abdulsalaam Arif was planning to lead a revolt against Abdulkareem Qasim, and he was jailed. Abdulkareem wanted Iraqis to have opportunities, to be able to obtain jobs and positions through competition and not through partisan alliances and favoritism.

Thus, Turkmen's hate continued to grow against Kurds. The Leader Abdul Kareem Qasim put Ibrahim Al-Nafitchi in person who was Turkmen rich and former deputy in Iraq at the previous King era. Qasim, a leader who had emerged in 1958 after the revolution, said" If there is any Ottoman soldier in Iraq, and then he has to leave Iraq immediately". (Note: Nafitchi family members numbered not more than ten people. Two brothers Hussein and Hassan had obtained a lease from the Ottoman Empire to sell black oil, which was on land surrounding the fire Baba Gur-Gur, in Kirkuk. Their sons were Ibrahim and Qasim. Their male relatives were Younis, Ramzy, and Yawuz—and they had a few female relatives.

I was fourteen when Ibrahim Beck was released from prison, and I went with boys from the neighborhood to the outskirts of the Ibrahim Al- Nafitchi property. He and his brother Qasim were sitting at the front of the house, and a black Rolls-Royce car was parked in front of Ibrahim Beck's house. We could see two huge Germans dogs and Uncle Salih the coffee server. We do not know if Uncle Salih was Kurdish or Turkish. He was short and relatively thin, and wore Turkish Ottoman trousers and red Yemeni shoes. The coffee pot and cups in his hands glittered, as he poured coffee for Ibrahim Beck and his brother Qasim Beck. Uncle Salih was an unmarried mad man, but God seemed to have created him to become the Nafitchi family's coffee server. Uncle Salih went to Hajj on his pilgrimage, to thank God

Taha in sixth grade and Mullah Mustafa Barzani

Our Kurdish leader Mullah Mustafa Barzani returned from Russia to Baghdad in 1958, and after a period of time he came to visit Kirkuk and was invited to Iraqi Officers Club.

I was in grade six at the time, when a Turkmen, a fellow student in my class, told a group of students, "Today one Turkmen soldier will shoot Mullah Mustafa Barzani, the leader of Kurds, from the military headquarter building, when he goes out from the military officers club in Kirkuk." The school day had not yet started, and I went home immediately and told this assassination news to my father, and he contacted his brother, Ali Basty. They then contacted Mullah Mustafa in the military officers club, and he was led to safety out the back door, which was on Atlas Street.

He then went to the Kirkuk military airport, flew to Mosul, and then took a car to the Barzan area. On the trip between the officers club and the Kirkuk military airport, the Turkmen commander, Major Hidayat Arsalan, had a heart attack and died in his military vehicle, on October, 25, 1958. But who knows how he really died, since a Turkmen writer later wrote, "Hidayat Arsalan was the first Turkmen martyr; he sacrificed his life for his country and his people."

Turkmen and Kurds become scapegoats

This hostility between Kurds and Turkmen did not affect my relationships with my Turkmen friends. We formed a sports team, and pooled our money to buy lumber and wood sheets. We tried to make a table tennis slab, but we failed. We had no experience, and the ball would not bounce on the poor table. We also tried to make volleyball net with some strings, and that effort also failed. The volleyball simply passed through the net, not over it. My group of friends often walked out of Kirkuk, to picnic in the countryside. We once traveled a greater distance on our bicycles, carrying our food with us.

I completed sixth grade in June of 1959. I was enjoying my summer holiday, but this enjoyment would not last. Kurds were celebrating the first anniversary of the July 14 revolution. They didn't know that they had gotten fake promises from Prime Minister Colonel Abdulkareem Qasim and from his assistant, Maj. Abdulsalaam Arif. The fake message said that Arabs and Kurds were partners in Iraq.

On July 14, 1959, Kurds were on the march, and suddenly Turkmen (maybe enemies of Turkmen) began pelting the marchers with stones, and hurling harsh words at the Kurds. So a battle ensued, spurred on by foreign spies and traders who killed a number of Turkmen. My family, like others, stayed in the house after hearing about the battle. We visited a number of Turkmen families, vowing to protect one another if evil came to our houses, but it did not, and our narrow alley remained peaceful.

Kurds were not fighting; they were only demonstrating to obtain their rights. They were not supporting Abdulkareem Qasim and his system. Following the attack, all Kurds left the crowds and remained at home, except for a small group who were under the control of political hunters. But some Turkmen and Kurds continued to fight. Some Kurds belonged to the Communist Party and some to the Kurdish Democracy Party. Others had no party affiliation. And some other Kurds did not belong to any parties. Iraqi military officers who were part of the British spy system got involved in a serious fight. They had their own goals and were prepared to fight for them.

The military officer in charge (he was Assyrian) ordered soldiers to drag the bodies of dead Turkmen down Kirkuk's streets and hang them from trees. Soon after the military officer gave that order, he fled from Kirkuk to an unknown place. This kind of fighting and killing, and the dragging and hanging of dead bodies is forbidden in Islam and all religions. These bad actions were not committed by all Kurdish people, but Turkmen blamed all Kurds for the fight, on July 14, 1959.

That fight did not serve the interests of either the Turkmen or Kurds, but it benefited other countries (Turkey, and Syria). I am sorry that twenty-eight Turkmen were killed in that fight. They didn't know what the fight was really all about. Otherwise, they would not have been involved. Turkmen and Kurds were like brothers in the city of Kirkuk.

The Turkmen served as a tool for Turks in Kirkuk to deny Kurds their rights. Turkey did not want the Kurds in Iraq to have any rights, for they feared that Kurds in Turkey would then also want their rights, and Turkey did not want to allow that. Egypt and Syria had a bad relationship with the Prime Minister, Abdulkareem Qasim, because he had not agreed to join the Arab Union (Egypt and Syria). Syria ordered the Ba'ath party to form a political relationship with Turkmen, to oppose the Kurds.

This added gas to the fires between Turkmen and Kurds, but the goal was to move Arabs into Kirkuk, and topple Abdulkareem Qasim from power, and get Kirkuk's petrol, and prevent Turkmen to be Turkey's spies. This would allow them to give control of Iraq to the Arab Union, which opposed Turkey and West. Arabs decided they did not wish to be under Turk control any longer.

Also, Abdulkareem's regime was described as communistic. He canceled the Baghdad Pact. The English were in control of the Iraqi Petroleum Company (IPC), and they developed a plan to increase the Turkmen's hatred of Kurds, by ordering some Christians and spies in IPC to join the Iraqi military. Abdulkareem Qasim ordered his military people to fight any opposition in Kirkuk, as he had in Mosul. Military officers and soldiers in Kirkuk used military trucks and vehicles to drag dead Turkmen bodies along streets.

The main goal was to create vandalism in Iraq, especially in Mosul and Kirkuk, and to topple Abdulkareem's regime. The English used some Christians (Teyyaries), because had used them during the World War I as mercenaries. When the English established the IPC, the petroleum Company in Kirkuk, they hired mostly Teyyaries and other Christians from Zakho, Silopi in Turkey, and some Christians from Iran. The IPC sent many Christian workers to London for training. They became high ranking staff people and engineers for IPC. The English constructed a new and modern city for them and named it Arafa City (New Kirkuk), and it was really a nice city, modern like a city in the United Kingdom.

Anyway, all four countries succeeded in increasing the hatred of Turkmen toward Kurds. After the fight, Abdulkareem Qasim changed his mind and turned against those who had fought Turkmen. He arrested and jailed many Kurds, and also gave a green light for Turkmen to assassinate Kurds in Kirkuk. This was a big mistake on the part of Abdulkareem Qasim and Turkmen. All Kurds' lives were in danger in Kirkuk between July 1959 and February 1963. It all prompted me to begin thinking deeply about freedom for Kurdistan.

Ch. 08- Taha at Middle School: 1959-1962

Taha at grade seven (1959-1960)

I began attending middle school (grade seven) in September of 1959, and I soon learned that I had ability in mathematics and Arabic. I liked sports, and I participated in the school's athletic activities. The Turkmen expressed strong hostility toward the Kurds at the school and in the city of Kirkuk. The Ba'ath party leaders secretly used the Turkmen as a tool. They conducted training sessions in Mosul (Iraq) and in Syria, providing instruction in how to kill innocent Kurds. I heard from some young Turkmen boys that Turkey was also sending Turkmen criminals to Germany for training in how to assassinate Kurds on the streets of Kirkuk.

Two young Kurdish brothers, originally from Sulaymaniyah, resided in our area. They owned a small shop that sold yogurt and cheese. They were calm and polite individuals, interested mainly in working and making a living. One morning as they were opening their shop, they were confronted by six Turkmen, who attacked them with fists, sticks and screwdrivers. One Turkmen attacked one of the brothers with a screwdriver, causing him to fall into a nearby stream. The other Kurdish brother was able to wrest the screwdriver from the Turkmen. He delivered a blow to his head, and the attacker fall to the street.

Onlookers were afraid to interfere, and one of those onlookers was me. I was fourteen years old, thin and weak, but in my heart I was pulling for the two brothers. Finally, some unknown individual fired a gun into the air, causing the uninjured Turkmen to flee. That individual, a Turkmen, had a compassionate heart; had he not fired his gun, those two Kurdish brothers would have died on the spot. The two brothers hovered between life and death, their only mistake being that God created them Kurds. These attacks continued between July 20, 1959, and February 8, 1963. The Turkmen were the tools, and the Kurds were the victims, but the main objective was to topple Abdulkareem, allowing the Ba'ath party to assume power in Iraq, and to deny Kurds their rights.

Ba'ath attempt to assassinate Abdulkareem Qasim

On October 7, 1959, Ba'ath assassins attempted to kill Prime Minister Abdulkareem Qasim, on Rasheed Street in Baghdad, using machineguns. Abdulkareem Qasim was consequently admitted to Al-Salam Hospital, but he survived, and he left the hospital December, 15, 1959. He then ordered the release from jail of all those who had been captured following the assassination attempt. But the Ba'ath officials hadn't changed their objective; they still wanted to assassinate Abdulkareem Qasim and take over the country of Iraq.

Following Abdulkareem Qasim's release from the hospital, Turkmen seemed to celebrate his survival. At the same time, however, they were cooperating with his enemies: the Ba'ath party of Syria and Egyptian party called Qawmee. Meantime, Turkmen continued killing Kurds. This assassination era in Kirkuk did not deter me from pursuing my education, and I easily

68

passed seventh grade. I struggled with the discrimination shown against the Kurds, but I excelled in grade seven, and I received the card that showed my scores.

Kurdistan revolution in Iraq

Kurdish leader Mullah Mustafa Barzani and other Kurds confronted Abdulkareem Qasim, the prime minister of Iraq, and demanded that he stop the assassinations of Kirkuk's Kurds. Then, on September 16, 1961, the Kurdish revolution began.

I started grade nine at the same middle school, and I was so proud that my father's and mother's tribes were participating in the revolution. I too became part of the revolution, working inside Kirkuk in a very secretive way. Arabs were coming to Kirkuk from Baghdad and Mosul, taking over Kurds' homes and taking their jobs. The Turkmen were killing Kurds, one at a time on the streets. They were assassinating Kurds in broad daylight, in front of citizens and Iraqis. They seemed to be without shame, and they seemed not to fear the wrath of God Almighty.

Turkmen were not just taking lives; they were also demolishing houses and destroying futures. In March of 1962, one rich Turkmen, Muhammad Sirajaddin, paid the mayor of Kirkuk $1,200 for permission to establish a new street, one that damaged our house and front yard, since both became part of the street. The rich man wanted the street to pass through the middle of his property, so that he could construct business buildings on both sides. He was a cowardly man, but a clever one.

On June 2, 1962, four members of the Turkmen mafia put four gunshots into my brother Sittar (Peshmerga). The shots did not kill him, and he was taken to the hospital, where a Kurd doctor, Abdulkadir Talabani, performed surgery. The next day, a nurse gave him a poisonous injection, which killed him. My father was a witness to the lethal act. The nurse was the same one who had wrapped my broken leg in the Kirkuk hospital, in 1953. He was good a good Christian man by the name of Rafael, who had been ordered by a Turkmen, Dr. Riza Tahir (director of health department in Kirkuk) to kill my brother Sittar. The nurse, Rafael, was powerless to resist the Turkmen mafia at that time, and I did not blame him for killing my brother. He too was a victim.

On the day that my brother was shot, I was taking a ninth grade test, the first day of a week-long Iraqi National Test (Bachelor Test) in Arabic. I did not quit— and I passed and moved on to tenth grade. My brother Sittar had left behind a family in Erbil, a wife and four kids. The oldest son was four years old and handicapped. We wanted to find them and tell them that Sittar had been murdered, but we didn't know their address, and neither family had a phone. So, my father and I went to Erbil, three days after my brother's funeral, to find them.

We joined others in a car that was transporting people between Kirkuk and Erbil. The driver dropped us off at a public transportation point, in the center of Erbil. We went to a teashop and ordered two istikans (containers) of tea. Then my dad said to the tea shop owner, "Please do you know where Sittar Muhammad's house is? He is from Kirkuk and has a wife and four kids.

The owner replied, "What is the name of the creek where his house is located?" My father said he didn't know. My dad then asked other customers in the tea shop the same question, but no one knew the location of the house.

At noon, we went to the mosque to pray, and after the prayers my father asked the mullah if he knew where my brother lived. The mullah also said he didn't know. We asked other teashop owners if they knew where we could find my brother, but no one could help us. We then went to pray Al-Asir (about one hour before sunset) in another mosque, and my dad asked this mullah if he knew where we could find my brother, but again no luck. My dad, who was getting older, grew weary and began to lose hope. He said to me, "I am going to take a nap; I am very tired."

He then went to sleep on a bench outside a teashop, and there were no customers in the teashop. My father then proceeded to take a ten-minute nap, as I watched over him, while surveying the area around the teashop. He suddenly awakened and said, "We are close to sunset. Let's go the public transportation point and return to Kirkuk."

A man then approached us and said, "I am seeing that you are not from Erbil and that both of you are so tired. Can I ask, what is your issue here in Erbil?" We described our sad situation, telling him that Sittar had been murdered and that we were here to take his family back to Kirkuk. He understood our problem, and we learned that he supported the Kurdish revolution. He told us to follow him, and we began walking from street to street and from creek to creek. Suddenly he said, "This is the house, the one in which Sittar rented only a room." We thanked the man, and asked God to save him. Sittar's wife and four kids then spotted us and greeted us with kisses and hugs.

I had an emotional reaction, and tears streamed from my eyes. My brother's widow looked as though she was expecting sad news. "What is going on," she said? Why are you are crying?" My dad then told her that Sittar had been killed in Kirkuk, and she began screaming and crying loudly, while also beating herself and rolling around on the dusty front yard. The neighbors came to the house and tried to assist her, but her emotions were out of control. She began grabbing mud and dust and slapping her head, behavior that frightened the kids, and they began to cry. They ranged in age from one month to four years. They did not understand that their father had been killed. It was the saddest moment in my life–I was about eighteen at the time.

The Kurdish neighbors prepared food for us and stayed with us late into the night. They also provided beds and a place to spend the night. Early the next morning the neighbors came to the house; and we gave them money to rent a vehicle (a Land Rover) so that we could transport blankets, mattresses, cloths, pots, and dishes back to Kirkuk. We left that morning, saddened by the tragedy that had befallen this young family. We knew that there were similar stories within the Kurdish community, as Turkmen continued to assassinate Kurds.

It was a big mistake for Kurds and Turkmen to begin fighting. Others used the conflict to their advantage. I hope the Kurds and Turkmen will, as before, again become one family in Kirkuk. Many of them are related to one another.

Following the military takeover, Abdulkareem Qasim installed Turkmen to head important government offices in Kirkuk. His people also got support from the Iraqi government, and from Turks, Syrians, Egyptians— and English officials in the petrol company—to kill Kurds in Kirkuk. The Turkmen of Kirkuk maintained good relations with Kurds in Sulaymaniyah and Erbil, a way of concealing their crimes against the Kurds in Kirkuk.

Turkmen continued to kill innocent Kurds on the streets of Kirkuk. The victims were unarmed, and never knew that they were targets of an assassination. Many members of my tribe were killed in that cowardly fashion. I knew that some Turkmen families had ordered the assassination committee to kill certain Kurdish neighbors, just out of personal hatred of them. Abdulkareem Qasim had give assassins a green light to murder Kurds in Kirkuk and Mosul.

I passed ninth grade, and I decided to work hard within the KDP party. I listened each night to the Kurdish revolution radio broadcasts. The revolution was weakening Qasim's regime, and the Ba'ath party was standing by, waiting for the right time to wrest control, to occupy Kirkuk, to force Turkmen to stop killing Kurds, to stop taking orders from Turkey, and to stop interfering in Iraq. Those killers did not include all Turkmen, only those cowards who bowed to the demands of Arab Ba'athists.

Iraqi officers and Taha at age sixteen
One day when I was sixteen years old, I was walking along Texas Street in Kirkuk, going toward Republic Street. I looked to my left and inside the branch leading to the Shatorlo creek I spotted about a dozen Iraqi officers, no enlisted men. They were 100 yards away from me and their uniforms were green like the color of a frog, and their shoulder patches and berets contained red lines. They looked like parrots from India or Pakistan. I stared at them for a time out of curiosity. I was not attempting to spy on them. I simply wanted to see what was going on in this part of my city.

Suddenly one officer spotted me, and he ordered another officer from his "parrot team" to arrest me. That officer ran toward me, followed by three more officers. I began to have thoughts of murder and assassination—and images of a bear chasing down a deer. I began to run, like a deer running away from a lion. These officers seemed to resemble wild dogs, not brave lions. Why, I thought, would they want to capture a teenager?

While I was running, I said to myself, "What has happened! Has the Third World War begun! Am I like a Jew in the Holocaust, running from the predatory Hitler dogs?" Then I realized that these Iraqi Arabic officers saw me as a Kurdish spy, a member of the Kurdish nationalism movement, and they were prepared to chase me down and harm me or kill me. The second officer neared me and tried to grab me, but I tripled my speed. My old shoes, one-year-old, had holes in the soles, which helped me make contact with the smooth ground. The officer then tripped and fell onto the cement sidewalk, looking like a scorpion or a turtle that had rolled over on its back.

He had been unable to capture me, even though he had much military training. Maybe he lacked holes in his shoes, which prevented him from maintaining contact with the cement sidewalk. A third officer began to chase me, but I kept running, and he finally fell on top of the second officer. With the help of God, I increased the distance between me and them, and I survived. Fortunately, there were no other soldiers on Texas Street, or in front of me. Otherwise I would have been ensnared in their trap. I survived physically, but the event hurt my soul. Afterwards I would have nightmares that I was running from them, and that they were relentlessly chasing me.

Taha and the art dream

In July of 1962, I passed grade nine. I tried to escape the injustices of the hunters and murderers by applying for admission to the Baghdad Institute of Fine Arts. I wanted to become an art teacher. Mr. Mahmoud Al-Obeidi, who was the art director of the Kirkuk Education Department, administered a test to thirty students. Fourteen passed, and I was one of them. The next week those students went to the Institute in Baghdad to take a final test. Only one student was chosen, and I was not that student. I returned to Kirkuk, and decided that after completing tenth grade I would apply to military aviation school.

Taha at high school

After my failure to be accepted at the Fine Arts Institute, I signed up for the tenth grade science class, and started the next school year. The principal was Mr. Akram Arslan, and I had a number of excellent teachers, including Mr. Muhsin Abdulhameed, a Kurd who taught Arabic language classes.

The school was close to an Iraqi military air force base in Kirkuk, and the planes would fly over the school, carrying petroleum bombs to drop on Kurds, who were struggling to attain self-determination and a better life. I would hear the planes, but I would stay focused on the teacher's explanations and on my lessons.

Newroz the national Kurdish feast day

There once was an unjust Kurdish king, Dhohak, who ruled over a Kurdish empire that stretched from Afghanistan to Bughdan (Baghdad). This king, according to legend, would carry two snakes on his shoulders, and each day he would feed them the brain of a young boy. Each family was required to bring a male child to King Dhohak's palace, to feed the snakes, and then they would return to their homes in a state of deep sadness. The King would order his executioner to kill the boy, open his head, remove the brain—and then place special parts on two gold plates, equal parts on each plate. The king would then feed his snakes, while enjoying this horrific crime.

One day in the year 612 B.C., the blacksmith Kawa was ordered to deliver his son to the king, for snake food. Kawa came to the palace, waving at the king as though he were slavishly following his orders. But as he neared the king, he removed a hammer from his shirt sleeve and struck the king's head, killing him. Those who had accompanied Kawa also carried hammers, and they struck fear into the hearts of palace guards, who were afraid to intervene, fearing for their lives.

The rebels, led by blacksmith Kawa, trekked to the mountains surrounding the palace and lit fires, and the fires of revolution swept across mountain peaks from Afghanistan to the Balkan Mountains, from the north to the south, from the east to the west, all in one night. The fires were a declaration of revolt against the tyrant King

Dhohak, and they signaled a brighter day for the Kurdish nation and other nations in the Kurdish empire.

This story was told to me by an educated Afghanistan individual. He said that Dhuhak and Kawa's graves can be found in the city of Jalal Abad, in Afghanistan. I see clearly that Kurdish borders stretch from Afghanistan through Iran, ending at the city of Khanaqeen, near Baghdad. Their multiple dialects consist of Beshto, Persian, Badini, Suarni, and Hawrami—all branches of the Kurdish language. Those who speak these dialects should study history and strive to develop a spirit of cooperation among themselves, while working to instill cooperation and love among all nations.

The Ba'ath and Jamal Abdinasir group revolution
I was doing very well at school, and I had completed the first half of grade ten, before going on winter school vacation. Ba'ath and Qawmee parties, working together had toppled the prime minister of Iraq, Abdulkareem Qasim, in Baghdad, on February 8, 1963. Ba'ath and Qawmee leaders executed Qasim, and they released Abdulsalaam Arif from jail and named him president of Iraq.

Ba'ath officials ended the Turkmen's killing of Kurds in Kirkuk, since both the Ba'ath and Abdulsalaam groups had reached their goal in Iraq. The Turkmen had only served as a tool for reaching that goal. Unfortunately, the Turkmen then became mercenaries for the Ba'ath party named Haras Qawmee (National Guard).

Abdulsalaam Arif's era and Kurdish village looting

In the second half of the school year, I began my tenth grade year. The Ba'ath and Qawmee groups had become brutal. They began occupying Kirkuk and working at the oil company (IPC). They would arrest Kurds who were working at the company, accusing them of being communists and Kurdish Democratic Party members. Many Turkmen were serving as agents for the Ba'ath party and Abdulsalaam Arif, spying on Kurds in Kirkuk.

As the second half of the school year began, I thought I might be arrested. A server for the Nafitchee Turkmen family, an Arab from an unknown village, would try to pick fights with me. But I kept my distance from this criminal. He was a mercenary, being paid by the Nafitchee family, who resided in my creek. He always carried a rifle; he was a coward who used a weapon to frighten others.

In March, 1963, Abdulsalaam Arif formed a group of Arab mercenaries. Many Iraqis called them Juhoosh, meaning donkey babies. The mercenaries were placed in the Iraqi army, with some Turkmen Ba'ath and Haras Qawmi members, to fight against the Kurdish revolution.

The Iraqi government under President Abdulsalaam Arif destroyed my village, Panja-Ali, in

Kirkuk, and also destroyed the villages of Shoraw, Daraman, Majeed Shana-Sheen, and Nabi Awa. Ba'ath and Qawmi people attacked Kurdish villages north of Kirkuk and looted the properties. They then burned the villages.

One day, after Kurdish forces had learned that inhuman acts of barbarism were being committed against innocent Kurdish villagers, Kurdish rebels organized a strike force and cut the road between the cities of Kirkuk and Hanjeera-Rash. (It was called Qara-Injeer: Turk Ottomans changed the name from Kurdish to Turkish). When forty Ba'ath mercenaries came back from the villages of Hanjeera-Rash, Kurdish forces in Iraqi military uniforms forced them onto a side road behind a hill and killed all except one, an individual they saved to serve as an eye witness, and to report the atrocity to President Abdulsalaam Arif. Thus, God punished them in this world for the shame they had inflicted on Muslim-Kurdish women. The news of the killing of the thirty-nine Juhoosh people reached the Iraqi government people, and they retaliated, behaving like animals and attacking defenseless Kurds in Kirkuk. My father, my brothers, and I were at risk, but escaped the violence.

I was in the second half year of grade ten. Ba'ath military officers had done shameful things to a group of thirty female high school students in Kirkuk, thinking they were training to fight against the Kurdish revolution. The girls were actually Haras Qawmi, allied with the Ba'ath party against the Kurds in Kirkuk. By their shameful attack, the Ba'ath party proved that they

80

did not mean to maintain respectful relations with Turkmen. They were only using them as a tool to control Kirkuk. God waits, but does not neglect.

I passed the tenth grade, but the Iraqi Military Aviation School had changed its admission standards, accepting only students who had finished eleventh grade, not tenth grade. So I decided to continue on to eleventh grade, the final high school year in Iraq. I was looking forward apprehensively to events on my summer vacation of 1964.

Teenagers hit by bamboo stick and Taha narrowly escapes

After the unfortunate incident between Kurds and Turkmen, on July 14, 1959, the relationship between the Arabs and Turkmen became stronger. In February of 1963, the Nafitchy family hired an Arab armed guard to scare the Kurds.

There was in our creek a Kurdish man, Mullah Ahmed, Imam of Nafitchy Mosque. This good man spent his youth in this mosque, serving the Muslim religion and Muslims. Mullah Ahmed was unmarried, and he cared for the mosque's grove, which had all kinds of fruit trees that yielded pomegranates, oranges, limes, grapes, berries, and dates.

After the fall of Abdulkameem Qasim, the Nafitchy family expelled this religious man, simply because he was a Kurd. He was seventy years old and had no other source of income. My father gave him

81

money to hire a man with a wagon, and he placed his humble belongings on the cart. My father also accompanied him to Shorjah creek in Kirkuk, to a small dark room where he awaited the journey of his pure soul from this temporary world to an eternal world. We school children eagerly awaited Mullah's departure, so that we could gather the grove's tasty fruits.

Mullah finally left, leaving behind fifty years of memories, and we children rushed through a small gate and into the grove, and began gathering fruit, competing with one another to see who could gather the greatest number of oranges and lemons. Suddenly, we heard an Arab voice, a scary voice that stopped us in our tracks. I stopped picking the fruit, and looked around for the source of the sound. I spotted the server Badir, the huge guard that the Nafitchy family had hired. He was holding a long bamboo stick, and was standing by the garden's only gate, prepared to beat us.

We young boys had no way to escape from the garden, since the grove had an only single port, a small door. All my friends were Turkmen, and I was the only Kurd. I devised a plan. I actually started to insult and beat my Turkmen friends, pretending that I was a member of the Nafitchy family. I could not tell my friends what I was doing, and they were hysterical, desperately looking for a way to escape. We looked like rats fleeing a killer cat. All the young boys ran at the guard and into him, hoping each would get only one or two hits, before hurtling themselves between Badir's two legs and escaping. I continued yelling—and insulting and beating my Turkmen friends until everyone had fled, leaving behind fresh fruits on the ground. They all received, however, more than two bamboo stick hits.

The monster Badir became confused and thought that I was a son of the Nafitchey family, since I was acting as though the grove belonged to me, and I was protecting it by beating the intruders. I filled my pockets with fruit and left, with no interference from Badir. I met my friends outside of the grove and told them what I had been doing. They laughed and congratulated me on my plan and the way I had avoided the blows of the despicable bamboo stick. Then I shared my fruits with my dear friends.

Ba'ath and Qawmee execute twenty-eight Kurds in Kirkuk

On June 23, 1963, Abdulsalaam Arif (Qawmee) and the Ba'athists executed twenty-eight Kurds in Kirkuk, revenge they said for the way Abdulkareem Qasim had imprisoned them, following a battle between Kurds and Turkmen in 1959. Some Turkmen people cheered the executions, as though the Ba'ath were exacting revenge for them. I passed from tenth grade in June of 1963 and I was happy, but the happiness did not last long, for a war had broken out between the Kurds and the Iraqi Ba'ath and Qawmee Abdulsalaam Arif.

It was a hot summer in 1963, and the Ba'ath party hanged the Kurd prisoners in the center of Kirkuk. Some Turkmen and Arabs celebrated around those

83

hangings, an inhuman act that is surely forbidden by any religion.

Ba'ath party and gypsy (Kawaly) girls

In the evening of June 23, 1963, on the day the hangings occurred, and as Ba'ath members and Turkmen celebrated the hangings, my Turkmen friends invited me to visit the Red Crescent Hall, which was also called the Red New Moon Club. My heart was filled with sadness and pain, thinking about the Kurds, but I went anyway, just to observe and see what was going on.

I entered the club with twelve of my eighteen-year-old friends, and I suddenly saw in the club hall semi-stripped ladies and depraved female dancers and singers. This wicked hall was full of Baghdad gypsy dancers. People of Turkmen and Arab Ba'aths were dancing with half naked dancers, and cigarette smoke was almost blinding the crowd of drunkards.

It was a shameful scene. It seemed as though they were celebrating the execution of twenty-eight Kurds. Oh God, it was shameful. How could one celebrate the death of others? This celebration was ordered by the Abdulsalaam Arif (the president of Iraq) group and Ba'athists. He was an evil leader. The journalist Abdulaziz Barakat asked him, "When will the Kurdish war have a solution?" He replied that Kurd rebels and Shiite soldiers were killing one another, and it was not his job to stop the fighting and solve the problem. He hated both the Kurds and the Shiites.

Abdulsalaam was well known for visiting places where Kawalies performed around his village. He always encouraged Iraqi soldiers to see this kind of low action, in order to disguise the disadvantages of war against the Kurds. For me, it was the first time I had seen half-naked women. I was torn between the enjoyment of seeing them and feelings of sadness for the executed Kurds.

While I was dealing with two opposing feelings, half-naked women came up to us and asked for a charity. I told myself, "Taha, leave now. This is not your place." I told my Turkmen friends that I was leaving, and in the blink of an eye, I was on the street, outside the Red Crescent Hall. Thank God that my father, Muhammad Jr., didn't discover that I had visited that awful club.

Those bad and sad actions by Ba'ath and Turkmen were daily conversational topics in Kurdish families in Kirkuk. I hated those injustices, and I tried to look at the sun and the moon to see if they could illuminate a path through the dusty bloody cloud that hovered over Kirkuk and Kurdistan.

I prepared myself for school, gathering together my two notebooks, two pencils, a sharpener, an eraser, and the rubber string to wrap around my notebooks. Yes, I prepared for the next level of education, while keeping Kurdish goals in my heart and mind. I knew God would do what he wishes for us, and I depended on Him.

Taha in eleventh grade (1963-1964)

In September of 1963, the final school year started, and I was prepared for the work ahead, in my science classes. I wanted to acquire the knowledge that would allow me to help my parents and the community—and to help myself.

I hated the sound of the Russian warplanes the Iraqis had acquired. I knew they were burning people in Kurdistan, people who only wanted freedom and independence, and relief from oppression. I was motivated by my love of education and my hatred of the warplanes. Love of education and hatred of warplanes seemed to go together, and it strengthened my conscience and my faith in God, a faith that I hoped would give me success in school and victory for the Kurdish people.

Taha and fight at high school (March 1964)
One day I heard a Ba'ath student, Haras Qawmi from Haweejah city, speaking badly about Kurds and Kurdistan. I asked him to stop, and he jumped out of his seat, prepared to fight. I immediately picked up a small piece of my broken class desk, a piece of wood that resembled a dagger. He saw that I was serious, and he ran away. I silently thanked him for running and perhaps saving me from a death penalty or maybe 100 years in jail. He went to a Ba'ath teacher, Nury Al-Rawee from Ramadee city, but our good teacher, Mr. Muhsin Abdulhameed, saved me from Mr. Al- Rawee.

Ba'ath people and President Abdulsalm Arif were trying to eliminate each. Ba'ath was tied to Syria, and Abdulsalaam was tied to the Egyptian leader, Jamal Abdulnasir. Each group was striving to gain more power. Abdulsalaam gave his tribe (Al-Jumaily) the authority to rule the government of Iraq. The tension between Ba'ath and Arif steadily increased, and the Kurds remained in conflict with both.

Abdulsalaam and Ba'ath Party

On November 18, 1963, Abdulsalaam Arif suddenly disarmed the Ba'ath party, and took over Iraq. Mr. Rawee and the Ba'ath student who hated Kurds left in my senior high school year, making my life more comfortable in the second half of that year.

My eleventh grade year was going well, and I was keeping up in my math, physics, biology, and Arabic classes. I was able to teach friends in my neighborhood. On Fridays I would teach five friends at school, using the black board and white chalk. It was illegal to enter school and to use the classroom without permission. But I was not doing it for myself; I was doing it for my creek friends, donating my time. The school had no guard on Fridays, so I able to teach and help my friends, which I enjoyed.

On June 1, 1964, after excelling in my classes, I took the General Ministerial Test, which I approached with confidence and hope. After a month or so, the test scores, which had been scored in Baghdad, were posted, on July 15, 1964. I got the results and almost lost my mind. They seemed so low. I said to myself, "Why has this happened? I had passed all the subjects except biology."

The scores did not seem to be mine; they were so below average. I was not alone in my concerns. My brother Musa also thought his scores were way too low. But we had no power, and we had to be patient in the face of treachery and hardship.

For a week or so I couldn't sleep, day or night. It was the summer of 1964; and my parents, brothers, and sister were sleeping on the flat roof of our house, but not me. I couldn't sleep. I just stared at the stars and thought about my educational future. I was planning to attend the civil engineering college at the University of Baghdad, but with this low (and incorrect) score, I knew I would not be able to pursue my desired educational future. Something had happened to my test notebooks and my answers to the Iraqi National Test (Bakaloria), but I didn't know the details.

I applied to Military Officers College

At the end of July, 1964, I applied to Military Officers College (MOC) in Baghdad. I spent a lot of time traveling between Kirkuk and Baghdad, and visiting MOC for interviews and all kinds of exams. I was tested on performances in running, swimming, jumping, and rope climbing. In the end, the security report against me from Kirkuk prevented me from being accepted by the MOC. I still had a goal, however; I wanted to learn the science and tactics of war, so that I could defend Kurds and repel enemies.

88

After the disappointment of failing to be accepted by MOC, I decided to attend The University of Baghdad, but I had no chance of being admitted to the Architecture College, because of my low (and incorrect) test scores.

Ch. 09- Taha and the University of Baghdad

First Year of College (1964-1965)

In the spring of 1962, we moved from Qoriah Creek to Almas creek in Kirkuk, where my two oldest brothers had bought a house. Our wealthy Turkmen landlord forced the move. We had lost half of our house, and had run out of rooms.

In September of 1964, after earning my high school certificate, I accompanied my brother, Musa, to Baghdad, to apply to the Educational College at Baghdad University. My brother and I had made the decision to attend the High Teacher Institution, after learning that we would not be admitted to the colleges of our choice—Medical College for Musa and Architectural Engineering College for me.

During my time in Baghdad, I came to realize that Ali Baba and the Forty Thieves were in power, and were stealing oil money that rightfully belonged to Kurds and Turkmen. Corrupt kings and presidents had been doing so since 1918. My brother, Abbas, was also residing in Baghdad, working for an American company as a welder and pipe instrument worker. He and my cousin, Fayzulla Khorshid, were renting a room in a relative's house in Hay Al-Thawra, in Baghdad. Abbas let us to stay in his rented room. We were four men in one room.

My brother Musa and I took a bus to college each day. The classes ran from 8:00 a.m. to 4:00 p.m. We ate

90

simple food served by the college, or we purchased food from road sellers, or from restaurants like Al-Jumhoriah, at the end of Rasheed Street, close to Maydan Square and to our college, in Waziriah in Baghdad.

After attending classes and filling our stomachs, we would return by bus to our room, where each of us had a simple mattress and a blanket. We had only water to drink, and no stove on which to make tea or fry eggs-- and no dishes or utensils. But I had a lot of recycled papers, which I had brought with me from Kirkuk to use in calculus, physics, chemistry, and biology classes.

The weather in Baghdad was good when we arrived, in September of 1964, but in December the nights turned cold, and our uncovered cement floor room seemed especially cold. One day my brother Musa, and my cousin Fayzulla, and I set up an empty oil metal container inside our room, and using wood scraps and pieces of scratch paper for fuel, we lit a fire. The flame nearly reached the ceiling, but we enjoyed the heat, for a time. Then my head began to spin and my stomach began to churn. I knew the source of the problem, and I said to Musa and Fayzulla, "The CO gas has entered my blood and I am going to faint."

I ran from the room, put my bag on the cement floor, and tried to fight off the fainting spell. I had no energy, and I took repeated deep breaths, trying to rid my blood of the poisonous CO. Poor Musa and Fayzulla could do nothing to help me. They removed the hot stove from the room, knowing that it could kill all of us. I knew then that I was safe, but the smell of CO lingered in our room for days.

I was hoping to easily complete my college degree and obtain a job as a high school math and physics teacher, a way of generating income that would support me, and that would also allow me to help my parents. My brother Musa was attending the same college, but he would not take a serious approach to his studies, and he finally failed, and returned to Kirkuk. I felt bad, but I knew why he failed. He wanted to be a medical doctor, but his low (and fake) high school score did not allow him to be admitted. We worried about his health. I became a top student, and I completed the first year of college, in 1964-1965.

Second year of college (1965-1966)
I started my second year in the fall of 1965; and I excelled that year in several subjects--math, physics, chemistry, and biology. The difficult part was trying to continue with empty pockets. My oldest brother in Kirkuk was able to send me ten Iraqi dinars each month, and I appreciated that help. I ate simple and cheap food, always trying to economize. I was not thinking about entertainment. I just wanted to get my degree, get a job, and help out my parents.

November came, and the weather turned cold, and I bought a jacket from a second hand store, in Shorjah market center on Rasheed Street in Baghdad. I liked its color, size, and price—but not its age. It was not my first choice. I remember the price--(7/20) dinar. The owner wanted to put it in a paper bag, but I told him there was no need for the bag; I would just wear it.

The next day, at the college, as I was happily awaiting the start of class, a beautiful girl approached me and said, "Congratulations Taha on your new jacket"
I said to her, "Thank you, but how do you know that it is new?"
She smiled, growing more attractive by the minute, and said, "I was in the bus, and it stopped in front of the second hand store, and I saw you trying on the jacket." I was a young man and shy, and my face turned red. She then changed the subject to math issues.

My Kurdish future was uncertain, and I knew I would have to help my parents. Moreover, I was in secret contact with my brother, who was my partner in the PDK, the Kurdish political party. If Iraqi security police were ever to learn about my PDK connection, I was ready at any time to leave the university and to join the Kurdish revolution,

All during my second college year (1966), the president of Iraq, Abdulsalaam Arif , continued the war against our Kurdish revolution, refusing to recognize Kurds' rights in Iraq. Unfortunately, Jalal Talabani, split from the Kurdistan revolution; and Abdulsalaam Arif used him of attacking the KDP party. Some Kurds joined the Jalal Talabani group, but only to obtain positions in Kurdistan areas that were under the Iraqi government's control. It was sad situation in Kurdistan. Military conflict broke out, and assassinations began to occur between Kurdish revolutionaries and Jalal Talabani's group.

In January 1966, I returned to Kirkuk for my winter school vacation, but my creek friends (all were Turkmen) asked me to cancel my vacation and take them to Baghdad. I agreed and we went as group of five. I took them to various places in Baghdad, such as the Baghdad museum, the zoo, the Hanging Bridge (Al-Jisir Al-Muallaq), Al-Nasir cinema, Al-khayam cinema, Rasheed Street, Abu Nuwas, and Games City (Madeenat Al-Alaab).

On the evening of the third day, my friends and I visited Bab Al-Sharjee in Baghdad. We were standing near the wagon of a vendor who was selling boiled chickpeas. There were many wagons and hundreds of people gathered about, eating a variety of hot winter foods--chickpeas, boiled turnips, eggrolls, and all kinds of sweets. It was a festive atmosphere. Large crowds milled around, and the sounds of radio music and vendors hawking their wares filled the air.

We were all enjoying the food and the happy surroundings, when I spotted danger in the form of a tall, broad shouldered individual, who was throwing punches at someone. But to who? I put my chickpeas bowl on the bandwagon and moved closer, and saw that it was my friend Fahraddeen. I said to myself, "Why did I expose my friends to this—people who are strangers in Baghdad?"

I wanted to help my friend, Fahraddeen, but I was feeling weak. I had been surviving on simple poor food, and I lacked the strength to oppose this villain. I thought to myself, even if I were to hit him from behind with a few punches, would that stop him? My hands felt weak, like biscuits, and I feared he would punch me senseless. Then without thinking, I yelled, "Sergeant, arrest that man," and the brutal giant instantly fled. I immediately checked out my friend, Fahraddeen, to make sure that he was not seriously injured, and that ended our time in Baghdad. The next day my friends traveled to Kirkuk, carrying with them stories of their short visit to Baghdad, the city of Ali Baba and the forty thieves.

I learned later that the huge violent man thought we were soldiers and army officers. In Iraq, at the time, a civilian who got into a fight with a military man would be attacked by other military men. So, civilians found it wise to retreat and not risk being confronted by military people, who would always protect one of their own.

Anyway, a few days after that incident, I resumed my studies in Baghdad, and began the second half of the school year. I told my friends about my encounter with the brutal giant, and how I made him run away like a scared rat. My friends, including a beautiful female classmate, laughed until tears rolled down their cheeks.

Abdulsalaam and Abdulrahman Arif
On April 13, 1966, the Iraqi radio broke into its regular programming to announce the death of

Abdulsalaam Arif, the president of Iraq. The Baath party had placed a bomb in his military helicopter, and it had detonated and killed him in the air, on his way to Basra province in the south of Iraq. The Baath party still did not have the power to replace the Iraqi government system, but it was one step forward for them. On April 17th, 1966, Abdulsalaam Arif's party installed his brother, Abdurrahman Arif, making him the president of Iraq.

While I stayed busy with my education, the new president of Iraq, Abdurrahman Arif, kept trying to solve the Kurds' problem. One day he visited the jail and met with my Uncle Ali, and he honored Uncle Ali and released him, because he had committed no crime. Moreover, he had prevented rapes, when English mercenaries had attacked women in Kirkuk, in 1924. Uncle Ali was in jail from 1959 to 1966.
Abdulkareem Qasim had arrested my Uncle Ali and put him in jail, in 1959, at age 65.

On May 1966, Uncle Ali moved from Kirkuk to Sulaymaniyah city, and tried to raise two of his grandsons, ages four "Azad" and five "Ilham". Their father had been hanged by Baath party officials, in Kirkuk, in the summer of 1963. Mullah Mustafa had sent him a letter of condolence, expressing regret for the execution Uncle Ali's son.

Uncle Ali died, however, and the two grandsons were left without a guardian. Fortunately, a ceasefire took hold between Kurdish revolutionaries and

Abdulrahman Arif's Iraqi military forces. Peshmerga (Kurdish freedom fighters) and Uncle Ali Basty's Manmi tribe people were in Sulaymaniyah, and Peshmergas carried his coffin. People in the street cheered his heroic actions, recalling the way he defended women in the public bath, in Kirkuk, in 1925, and being a Peshmerga leader in Kurdish war against English army at the era of Sheikh Mahmoud from 1925 to 1931.

I then returned to Baghdad to continue my studies, in spite of the presence of Kurdistan enemies. Abdurrahman Arif did not solve the Kurdish problem, mainly because the Kurd haters in Baghdad continued to undermine his problem solving efforts. I continued to pursue my studies in Baghdad.

Anyway, I passed the second year of college, remaining a top student, and I told my relative that I would no longer be renting a room from him in Hay Al-Thawra—it was too far away from the college. I then traveled to Kirkuk for summer vacation.

Third year of college (1966-1967)
One day, on my summer vacation, I spotted my brother Musa reading a book titled Stop Worrying and Start Life. I asked him about his educational plans, and he said that he was trying to gain admission to Medical College at Karachi University, in Pakistan. This was good news, and I was hoping he would reach his goal--to become a medical doctor. I recalled my mother being ill, and Musa as a sixth grader buying her medicine and vitamins. I recalled an amusing incident. He bought

97

vitamin B syrup for the entire family, and it turned our teeth black for a week. Toothpaste would not remove the stain.

In August of 1966, I returned to Baghdad, to look for a room. Two friends, Khaldoon Ali and Mohamed Ameen, and I found a room for three Iraqi dinars, in an old house that contained eight rooms. The house sat in a narrow, long, and zigzagging alley, which was contaminated by sewage. The old alley was in the Haydar Khanah area, perhaps built during the era of Harun Al-Rashid, or in the days when the Shah of Iran ruled, and Baghdad (Boghdan) was part of the Persian Empire. The entrance to the alley was located on the Al-Rashid Street, close to the Maydan Square.

Each room accommodated three or four students. We waited in line to use the morning bathroom, from which came foul smells and sounds. Our room had no air-conditioning and no heating systems. I had to constantly adjust my layers of clothing.

The college year began in September (1966), and I was looking forward to my math and physics classes. I had applied for University financial aid two years previous, and I was still waiting. Finally, in my third year, the University of Baghdad agreed to provide five Iraqi dinars per month—in the form of a loan. This small assistance (less than $2.00) allowed me to eat at restaurants for a few weeks.

One day, my parents suddenly showed up in Baghdad. They had come from Kirkuk via public minibus. They couldn't afford to own a car, and they were unable even to drive. They took a hotel room, which happened to be close to my rented room, although they weren't aware of that. We had no phone connection, but then they saw my friend, Khaldoon, near the hotel at Rasheed Street. Who knows how long my poor father waited at the hotel gate, hoping to see me or Khaldoon?

My parents and Khaldoon came to my room, and I was surprised and so happy to see them. I hugged them and kissed their hands. My dad was carrying a big pot of Iraqi food called doulma. They had brought it from Kirkuk because they knew it was one of my favorites. Baghdad's simple restaurants had no doulma, and we happily started in on it. My dear parents stayed in Baghdad for only one night, and then returned to Kirkuk.

Taha graduates from University

I graduated from the University of Baghdad in June of 1967. I was the top student in mathematics. The university canceled the graduation ceremony because of the Arab and Israel war, which had broken out on June 5, 1967. Thus, I did not receive my award, a gold watch.

The university asked graduates to attend a mandatory military training course, so I stayed in Baghdad for one month, training with the Youth Brigade. The University allowed us recent graduates to sleep at the student dorm, and we were each given ten Iraqi dinars per day, to buy food at the dorm facility. In the final days of training, I submitted my graduation document to the Ministry of Education in Baghdad, which handled the hiring procedure. I was to be assigned to a high school in Iraq as a math teacher. I did not have the right to choose the city or the school in which I would work.

On October 1, 1967, I returned to Kirkuk. I had been hired to teach math in Kirkuk province, and I assumed that the Education Department in Kirkuk would place me in the city of Kirkuk, since I had been a top college student. But Turkmen controlled the Kirkuk Education Department, and they assigned me to a small city called Chamchamal, which was in Kirkuk province. But I was happy to get the job, and to have income that allowed me to help my parents. My happiness increased when I heard that my brother, Musa, had been admitted to the Medical College, at the University of Karachi, in Pakistan.

Ch. 10- Taha: A Mathematics Teacher in Iraq

Chamchamal Middle School 1967-1968)

On October 15, 1967, I began teaching mathematics at the Chamchamal Middle School. I was young, but I was serious. I wanted to be a good teacher. I taught math, physics, chemistry, and biology for one year. The school was set in a small town, surrounded by farms. My relatives' villages were close by.

I was following our Kurdish revolution in a very secretive way, and my political contact was with my brother in Kirkuk. But it was a sad situation, sad to see Mr. Jalal Talabani's military group in Chamchamal cooperating with the Iraqi military against Kurdish leader Mullah Mustaf's forces at Abdulrahman—all during Arif's presidency. It was so sad to see the Kurdish freedom fighters so divided, and fighting one another. I feared for my life at times. I belonged to Mullah Mustafa's revolutionary movement, and I feared both the Iraqi military people and those in the Jalal Talabani group.

The school principal was apparently a communist and well known for his use of alcohol and interest in gambling. He may have been a spy on a communist. He was basically a client of the Turks, and his family opposed the Kurds in Erbil.

The school janitor and the principal possessed a bad set of ethics, and they had secrets. One teacher, a

Turkmen from Erbil, had a silly relationship with the principal. This teacher was immoral—and disaster prone.

There was an Iraqi army post in Chamchamal, and the principal and his bad teacher friend would attend meetings at this post. As for me, I would meet with a Peshmerga student named Aziz Abdulkadir, and he would give me news of the Peshmerga heroes who were being led by Mullah Mustafa Barzani. I would eagerly await this news, and I suffered when I heard about the martyrs who had given their lives to the cause. This student kept my Kurdish freedom movement activities secret. Otherwise, I would have been taken from this life and this world. I owe that student much (Aziz Abdulkadir), but I do not know what became of him.

I lived in fear that the Iraqi army forces would arrest me. The military and Jalal Talabani people were shelling Kurdistan, using Russian long-range aircraft and powerful guns. The military forces surrounded roads leading to the ports; and security and intelligence agents, police, and the mayor's people were constantly searching Chamchamal, trying to identify and arrest those who were backing the Kurdish revolutionary movement.

Taha's and Malika's Marriage
After I completed my first year of teaching, my mother said to me, "Hey, Taha, it is time for you to get married." I liked her message, but I replied, "Not yet, Mom." She said, "Yes, it is the time for you to have a wife, because I need to see your kids around me before I die." I said, "No, Mom. You will not die, because

without you we are nothing." She laughed at me and said, "Tomorrow I will go to my relative's house and talk to the hero, Khalid Agha." I said, "Why?" She said, "He has a beautiful young girl named Malika, and she is like a nice flower." I gave her permission to go and look at the girl, so that I could get a good description.

It was June of 1968. My bed was on the flat roof or our house, and I would lie there and dream about my life partner. The night would pass, and the sun's golden rays would touch my eyes. This day, however, would be different. After a short shower and a breakfast, I waited for my mother to leave, to visit Khalid Agha; and at 4:00 p.m., my mom and youngest sister left our house, and set forth.

They returned after three hours, and told me about Malika's beauty, and then told me about her parents and their tribe, which was my mother's tribe as well. I said to my mother, "I would like tomorrow to see her." My mother said, "Not tomorrow, but after one week, we will go visit Khalid Agha's house, and then you can see her and she will see you, too." My parents and little sister, Suhayla, then went to Khalid Agha's home a second time. They discussed a possible marriage, and they got permission from her parents for the two us to meet, me and Malika, at their house.

A week later, my mother, father, and my two sisters and I went to the hero Khalid's house, to visit. We knocked on the door, and a little five-year-old boy greeted us. We said, "Go tell your parents that we are visitors." Khalid and his wife, Talatt, and three little boys immediately came to the door and warmly invited us in. We stepped into the visitors' room, and suddenly I found that everyone had left: I was all alone in the room.

I was sitting on a rug—there was no chair in the room--and looking around nervously, when a girl appeared. I said to myself, "This is the girl I have to see now." My body started shaking, my face turned red, and it was so difficult for either of us to look at each other. She said to me, "Brother, welcome." She was carrying a glass of cold drinking water on a nice tray. She offered me the glass of water. My hand was shaking, and very shyly I took the glass of water from her tray.

I was unable to look at her face and her body. I had the glass of water in my hand, but my lips were shivering, and it was difficult to take sips from the glass; but I took a few sips and set the glass back on the tray, which she was still holding. When she turned to leave, I looked at her body, legs, and feet—in order to determine if I should say yes or no to the proposed marriage. I decided deep in my heart to say, "Yes, this is the girl Malika who was my dream." After this brief water meeting between Malika and me, my parents and her father came to the room. We thanked Khalid Agha for his hospitality, and then we left.

We arrived home, and my parents asked me, "Did you like her?" I very shyly said, "Yes, I liked her." My parents then went back to Malika's house to ask about her opinion of me. The response was positive, and her parents and my parents made the final agreement: we would be married. She and I had liked each other at first glance, at the water meeting. My parents returned and said to me, "Malika is yours, and you are Malika's." On June 1, 1968, a doctor signed the papers at the hospital, without checking Malika's blood or mine to make sure that we were fit for each other.

My sister and her mother bought clothes and gold for Malika. On June 6, 1968, there was a short celebration, conducted by women and kids at Malika's house, and at that time relatives and neighbors announced that Malika and Taha were in the process of marriage. On that day, the religious agreement was made at Malika's house. Her father was selected to represent Malika and to tell the Mullah, the Muslim religion's pastor, that Malika had agreed to become the wife of Taha.

Her father put a golden ring on my right hand finger, and my mom put a golden ring on Malika's right hand finger. A day later we made the official government marriage agreement. On July 12, 1968, my family and relatives rented cars, and we went to take Malika from her father's house. Of course, at her house and at my house, there were big feasts.

When my team's cars stopped in front of Malika's house, a group of young boys started throwing fruits, vegetables, and small rocks at us. Malika's little brothers each held a rock, and blocked the door, keeping me from taking Malika from her house. The situation was emotional for Malika, and dangerous for my team. I started throwing coins at the young boys, which distracted them, as they stayed busy picking up the coins.

I took Malika's hand, and we jumped into a nice car, which was decorated with balloons, colorful shiny papers, and flowers. We were a convoy, and we visited many major streets in Kirkuk before heading to my house. When we arrived at our house, more young men and kids were waiting, intending to make problems for us. I threw more coins on the ground, to get rid of the problems they were completing.

I have a great regret that I made a big mistake in that I did not allow my wife, Malika, to complete her education. She was sixteen years old, and I was a teacher, acting like a king. I thought it best that she stay at home and take care of herself and kids, since my salary could cover our needs. There was another reason I wanted her to stay home. I wanted her to avoid the difficulties of a work life. I wanted her to stay young forever.

Saddam and Ba'ath

On July 17, 1968, five days after of our marriage, Ba'ath party officials, including Ahmed Hassan Al-Baker, Saddam Hussein, and a faction from the Tikreet party, visited President Arif, ostensibly to drink coffee with him in the presidential palace. The president, poor man, could not foresee what they intended to do with this visit.

While drinking coffee, they captured him and told him to order his protective guards not to interfere. They further told him that he must surrender his presidential powers. The poor people of Iraq had no part in this decision. They were busy working at the jobs and caring for their families.

The Ba'ath party officials then expelled Arif, sending him to London. Unfortunately, Ahmad Hassan Al-Baker then became president of Iraq, and Saddam became vice-president. They announced the white revolution, but the Iraqi people would learn later these foxes were in fact vicious wolves.

Haweejah High School and teachers' attack (1968-1969)

The Ba'ath party transferred me from Chamchamal to the city of Haweejah, instead of letting me reside in Kirkuk. I rented a muddy house and took my wife, Malika, with me. Saddam was recruiting people into the Ba'ath party, often by giving them civilian jobs and military ranks. In Haweejah, some Arab people sold themselves to the Ba'ath party for certain benefits. Saddam arrested Sheikh Muzher Al-Ubaydi, because he would not bow to his party's demands. Sheikh Muzher was a prominent Arabic tribal leader, and he was a wise man. He had the ability to solve problems among the many tribes in the Haweejah area.

While in Haweejah some parents who were Sheikh Followers offered to give me gifts in the form of

their farm products. I refused to take the gifts. I knew
that they were not trying to bribe, and I knew that they
respected me, and I appreciated their offer. But I did not
wish to have any involvement with their gifts. Maybe I
was wrong, but I was a straight person. I knew that the
Haweejah students, in most school years, would attack
teachers who gave them a failing (F) grade. I was ready
for a possible attack, simply for giving some students
special help. I saw that my job was to teach well, and to
help a high percentage of students pass my classes.

Late in April of 1969, Jasim Khalaf Al-Ubaydi, a
Baath student, came to my door at home. His chest was
covered with belts of bullets, and it seemed that he was
trying to threaten me. He knew that he had some power,
and that I was an easy target—I was a Kurd and regarded
as a second class citizen. He demanded that I pass him in
two subjects: algebra and geometry. He was failing, but
he wanted these fake grades. I refused his demand. I
couldn't comply with his demand: I was an honest
man—honest with myself, my students, and my God.

**Malika, my unborn baby, and me—under a Ba'ath
student pistol attack**
    In May 1969, I was driving along in a car with
Malika, who was pregnant. I wanted to take her from
Haweejah to Kirkuk city. We rounded a curve on the
muddy road, close to the city of Riyadh, when suddenly I
spotted my Arab student, Jasim Khalaf, with a gun in his
hand, seemingly prepared to murder me. I said to
Malika, "This student wants to assassinate me. I will
drive very dangerously, and you must keep yourself

108

strong. Otherwise, we will die." She yelled and cried, but I said to her, "This will not help us; be quiet and let me use my mind."

She said, "Don't worry about me or my baby. Do what you see is safe for us."

I rolled down my window, and extended my arm, and said, "I will stop near you. I will stop when I get out of the mud." I acted as though I was about to stop, slowing the car to almost a halt. Our hearts were beating very fast, and I knew we were close to being attacked by this Arab Ba'ath student, Jasim Khalaf. He was ready to shoot, and his gun was in his hand. I began to open the car door, and then I pushed the gas pedal to the floor, causing water and mud to splatter all over the car—and all over the beastly student's body. I heard gun shots, but I kept weaving the car left and right until we were able to get behind a hill, and away from the gunfire. 'God saved my wife, the undelivered baby, and me from the Ba'ath student's bullets.

We made it to Riyadh, and I drove to the police station, which was close to the spot where we had been attacked. I reported the incident to the police officer, but then he proceeded to attack me with harsh language. He was a relative of the student. I then drove to the educational district office in Kirkuk, which was occupied by Ba'ath party officials, and again reported the incident. But an assistant superintendent (Lutfee Al-Tikrity) said, "You had better pass those students in Haweejah, for your own good safety."

I then traveled to Kirkuk to buy a handgun, to protect myself from killers. But there was no shop in Kirkuk that sold guns, and I had to find a gun smuggler, which I did. His name was Hussein, and he was a Kurd. I bought the hand gun, but it was a dangerous transaction. If caught by Ba'ath officials, I would have been jailed. Non-Ba'ath people were not permitted to possess a gun.

I left Malika in Kirkuk and traveled alone to Haweejah, where I learned that the police had arrested my attacker, the boy student. Later, his father came to my house and pleaded for peace. I respected him and his request, and told the police to release the boy.

The next day, at school, I attended a teachers' meeting in which the student gun attack issue was raised and discussed. I announced that I had forgiven the the student, Jasim Khalaf, but an Arab teacher, Ashraf Al-Doory (assistant principal) proceeded to criticize me for this act of forgiveness. I objected to his criticisms, and he approached me as though he was going to physically attack me. I picked up a chair to use as a defensive weapon, and he stopped, and I stopped. The teachers then decided to transfer the student to another school, for the next school year.

I finished out the school year and returned to Kirkuk on June 1, 1969, for my summer vacation. I moved my home furniture to Kirkuk. On June 6, 1969, our first baby son, Lukman, came into this world. I named him Lukman out of respect for Mullah, whose son was also Lukman.

I completed my summer vacation in Kirkuk, and returned to Haweejah to teach (1969-1970). This time I had a pistol, secretly concealed but ready to repel any attackers. I applied for a transfer, from Haweejah High School to Kirkuk, but this time Ba'ath party officials transferred me to the city of Dozkhormatoo. After one month, they transferred me to Alton, a city that was originally called Perdy, in Kurdish. The Ottoman Empire had changed its name to Alton Kopry, which means "Golden Bridge."

Altoon Kopri High School (1969)
I started teaching at Altoon Kopri High School in October of 1969. The city of Altoon Kopri was a half-hour drive from Kirkuk. Each day I would come and go, using the services of a Turkmen driver, an elderly and respectful and very intelligent gentleman.

Altoon Kopri city was divided by a river called Zaab Al-Sagheer. Kurds and Turkmen in Altoon Kopri were on friendly terms—they got along with one another. A famous man, Mr. Yawar, invited the school faculty to a huge dinner, at which he delivered some wise words. He was a positive leader, and he worked to develop a positive culture within the city.

The students were very cooperative, and I had a good teaching experience there. Mr. Taher Khorsheed, a teacher at Altoon Kopri Middle School, was from Altoon

Kopri. I invited him to join the Kurdish Democratic Party, but he declined the invitation, saying that his situation did not allow it.

On March 11, 1970, while teaching at the middle school, Saddam and Mullah Mustafa Barzani, the Kurd leader, agreed to stop the war and establish a ceasefire between the Iraqi government and the Kurds. The Kurdistan Democratic Party transferred me to Kirkuk, my city, to teach mathematics at Kawa Middle School.

Kurds and Saddam Agreement March 11, 1970

On September 20, 1970, the start of new school year, I reported to the Education District office in Kirkuk to get my new school order, for the Kawa Middle School in Kirkuk. I obtained my order, and I also volunteered to teach match at Imam Qasim and Shorja high schools in Kirkuk. They were Kurdish schools, and they needed math teachers. My teaching experience in Kawa was a good one, and the students appreciated me.

The Kurdistan Democratic Party (KDP) chose Ali Sinjary (he was from Sinjar city in Mosul province) to head the Kirkuk party branch. Then KDP sent Fahry Bamirly to head PDK headquarter in Kirkuk. I was doing my best as a teacher, while also working with the Party in after school hours. I would secretly ride my brother's bike to meetings, and I ran two cells of PDK party members. These party members consisted of staff people and workers at the petroleum company in Kirkuk city. My party boss was Kak Mohammed Barwari, from the city of Dohuk. His son was Azad Barwari.

112

The four-year ceasefire agreement guaranteed that Saddam would have no opposition. But he had not plans for a permanent settlement. The ceasefire simply gave him time to plan his murderous and oppressive strategies.

Ch. 11- Saddam: An Uneducated Devil

Saddam and the four-year cease fire

The dictator Saddam Hussein carried out the following actions:

1) Using the name Abu-Tabir, he killed secretly the individuals and families in Baghdad who opposed him.

2) He ordered all Iraqi male adults who had not served in the military to complete two years of military service— or else give his government 4,000 Iraqi dinars. I was one of those who chose to give money, in order to avoid serving in Saddam's criminal army. He collected billions of dollars, which he used to buy weapons and to hire gangs to protect him and support his regime.

3) He poisoned farmers' cows and sheep, causing citizens to stop eating meat for one year.

4) He nationalized the Iraqi Petroleum Company and confiscated half the salaries of all government workers.

5) He tried to kill all prominent leaders of the Kurdish revolution. In 1973, he sent three assassins from Baghdad to the city of Choman to kill Mullah Mustafa Barzani. God saved Barzani.

6) He bribed some Kurdish leaders, Aziz Aqrawee and others, to join him.

7) He persuaded Iraqi communists such as Al-Hajj and Mukarram Talabani to support his opposition to the Kurdish revolution.

8) He bribed Kurds to spy on other Iraqi Kurds.

9) He moved five thousand uneducated Arabs from villages in western and central Iraq to my city, Kirkuk. He allowed these mercenaries to reside at City Hall Club, called Baho Baladia. The toilet facilities were inadequate for that number of people, and the Arabs soiled the building and the surrounding areas. Many residents, prominent people such as doctors and lawyers, moved away from the City Hall Club area because they were unable to tolerate the stench and nor was I; I could not stand it when I tried to visit a place near the city hall club. Saddam was hoping that those Arab mercenaries would capture Mullah Mustafa and occupy Kurdistan.

10) He made connections with Eastern and Western countries and purchased chemical weapons and other military weapons.

11) He tried to persuade Arab countries to oppose the Shah of Iran. He made Tumbule-Sughra and Tumbul-Kubra islands in the Gulf a political issue.

12) He opposed Hafiz Al-Assad, the president of Syria, to show that he had power over other countries—and to frighten Iraqis into obeying his regime.

Kurdish people believed that Saddam would give them the rights they deserved. My brother, Musa, returned from Pakistan (he was attending a medical college in Karachi) to visit our family in Kirkuk, and to enjoy a summer vacation in Iraq. When he tried to return to his medical college, Saddam's security people stopped him at the Baghdad airport and told him that he had to join the Iraqi military forces. He tried to persuade the Iraq Ba'ath government officials to let him return to his medical studies, telling them that if he could not go back he would lose his opportunity to become a medical doctor.

He saw, however, that Saddam and his henchmen would not allow him to return to Karachi, so he contacted Kurdish revolutionary figures and met with the Kurdish leader, Mullah Mustafa, who helped him return to Pakistan. But it was sad to see the ways in which the Ba'ath party was denying Kurds their rights—and also denying other Iraqis their rights. My brother, Musa, fled Iraq; but the rest of us remained there, living in a state of fear and daily threatened by the Ba'athists. Saddam seemed determined to stamp out the Kurdistan revolution, led by Mullah Mustafa.

Saddam was a devil, and an uneducated one. He had been kicked out of elementary school in Tikreet, when he was a sixth grader, for trying to kill a teacher. He came to Baghdad to join his uncle, Khayrulla Tulfah, an Iraqi military officer. He became a gang member and joined the Ba'ath party, and then became involved with a group that was trying to assassinate Abdulkareem

116

Qasim, in Baghdad. Imagine how evil he was! He became vice president of Iraq in 1968, and signed an agreement with the Kurdish leader, Mullah Mustafa, to establish a ceasefire. But this agreement was only a tactic, a way of buying some time for him to arm his military forces. He had no intention of keeping the agreement, which was to last from 1970 to 1974.

Saddam and Kurds war (1974-1975)

Saddam's political strength rested heavily on his military strength, on his weapons. Mullah Mustafa clearly saw the dictator's objective. He wanted to dominate Kirkuk, which was in Mustafa's words "the heart of Kurdistan." Mustafa was determined to stand like a mountain against Saddam and his Ba'ath military forces.

In March of 1974, I prepared my family (my wife and four sons) to move from Kirkuk to Chamchamal, a city between Kirkuk and Sulaimaniah. I wanted to support my parent's tribes in their efforts to oppose Saddam and to back the Kurdish revolution. Unfortunately, that did not happen. My father had grown old, and both parents had had little income. I stayed in Kirkuk to care for them, even though I was threatened by my political enemies. I knew my life was in danger, but I felt a responsibility to care for my parents.

Saddam ended his ceasefire agreement with the Kurds in March of 1974, and then launched military operations against Kurdistan. Some Kurdish individuals had benefited from the ceasefire, and many did not wish to relinquish those advantages. They joined Saddam in his attacks against the Kurds. Other Kurds who had joined the revolution quickly returned to Saddam's side, to regain the benefits they had enjoyed during the ceasefire.

My views stayed the same. I remained loyal to Mullah Mustafa and the objectives of the Kurdistan revolution. I did not get any personal advantages from the KDP ceasefire, and I did not ask for any favors. My dad and I listened each day to radio broadcast reports about the Kurdish revolution, and we prayed for its success.

Some of the Kurdish opportunists held positions in official Kurdish offices, but they had also held similar positions given to them by the Ba'ath Party. Some had completed educational programs in Egypt, London, and the U.S.—and had served as branch members of the Ba'ath party, as had their sisters and wives.

Saddam's military forces had begun bombing schools, hospitals, and civilian locations in suspected revolutionary areas. Saddam used mercenaries, Kurdish militias called Jaash (meaning donkey's baby), regular Iraqi military forces, and Ba'ath militias called Jaysh Sha'abee. I was told that Kurds from my parent's tribes were heroically defending Kurdistan and resisting Saddam's brutality.

Kurds were becoming increasingly active in the resistance, in the conflict between Iraqi Kurds and

Saddam's regime. And yet, two sons of Mullah Mustafa continued to serve as ministers in Baghdad! I believe that both were being forced to serve, that they were being held as hostages.

After one year of heavy fighting, Saddam began to lose his supply of bombs and heavy weapons, and the Kurdish revolution began to grow stronger. This caused Saddam to reach out for help, to find allies who would support his murderous regime.

Shah of Iran and Saddam

In 1975, when Saddam realized that he was in danger, he met with the Shah of Iran, in Algeria, under cover of a supposed petroleum meeting. He asked the Shah for help in ending the Kurdish revolution. The Shah then invited Mullah Mustafa to Tehran, the capital of Iran, and told him to end the revolutionary activities— or he would join Saddam and help him end it. Mullah Mustafa had no choice, and he ordered Kurdish troops to stop their military activities. He gave the troops three options:

Kurds can return to their homes in areas under Saddam control.
Kurds can relocate to Iran.
Kurds can ask for refugee status in America and European countries.

The three options were set in place, and my father and our family members felt a great sense of sadness. The revolution had collapsed, and Saddam began ordering his assassins to kill Kurdish freedom fighters in Iran, Iraq, and Europe. All Kurds felt deeply disappointed and sad, especially my father: he died just a few months after the Shah joined Saddam's campaign to crush the Kurdish revolution.

Saddam also began sending thousands of selfish Arabs from southern and central parts of Iraq to "Arabize" my city, Kirkuk, and surrounding areas. He gave each of those families 10,000 Iraqi dinars, and he also endowed them with land, jobs, and various forms of power. He later raised the amount to 20,000 Iraqi dinars. It should be noted that many heroic Arabs refused Saddam's offers; they refused to move from their motherlands, where their grandparents lay buried, and to occupy other people's lands in Kurdistan.

Iraqi people identified those 10,000 Arabs who had accepted the 10,000 dinars, and Arabs in Kirkuk are still transferring their dead back to the cities from whence they came. Unfortunately, Arab and Ba'ath individuals took over directorship of Kirkuk offices and schools. They brutalized Kurds in Kirkuk. Shooting and hanging them, and preventing them from buying or selling houses and lands.

In July of 1975, I bought a new car, and after few months I sold it for a profit of 800 dinars. I was earning money by tutoring math outside of school, and 1 was staying alert for any Kurdish news I could find about the Kurdish movement. Following the collapse of the Kurdish revolution, a lot of secretive things began to occur. The Shah was driven from power, and Imam Khomeini took over. Mullah Mustafa traveled to America and met with the Shah for some kind of discussion.

Kurdish Revolution once again, 1976

In 1976, leaders in Kurdistan again began opposing the Ba'ath party, making it clear that the Kurdish revolutionary spirit was still alive. I was still a KDP member, but my heart was at the same time attracted to this new revolutionary movement, the PUK, led by Jalal Talabani. Saddam realized that Kurds were again revolting, trying to throw off the Ba'athist yoke of domination and oppression.

Meantime, my brother, Musa, had graduated from medical school in Karachi, Pakistan, and he had returned to Kirkuk, to serve as a medical doctor. Ba'ath officials, however, asked him to first carry out military service. He then contacted a high ranking Iraqi military officer in Kirkuk, who was able to save him from this mandatory military service.

In 1977, my family had accumulated some cash savings. My wife sold her gold, and with that we acquired some residential land, at a cost of 1,700 Iraqi dinars. I applied to register our land in the government office of deeds, but I heard nothing for several months. One day I took a technical petition to the mayor of Kirkuk, Waleed Al-Aedamee, and he agreed to register the land. He also gave me permission to build a house on it.

121

Saddam later had that mayor hanged, but we built our house, with the help of my older brother. I worked hard at my school teaching and at my private teaching, working to repay the money my brother had lent us for the house construction. It was my first house, and on June 1, 1977, my family and I moved into it, in Alams Creek, in the city of Kirkuk. Then, in 1978, we welcomed a new baby son into our family. We named him Rezgar. We now had five sons—no daughters.

Ch. 12- Planning an Escape

Turkmen Ba'ath teachers at Kawa Middle School

In 1979, my school was controlled by the Ba'ath party, and Ba'ath officials changed the name of Kawa Middle School to Ma'ad Bin Jabal Middle School. The murderous Ba'ath party wanted to hang me—that is, execute me—because of political charges made against me by the school's Turkmen Ba'ath teachers, and one other individual.

That other individual (a teacher), I regret to say, was a Kurd. He had organized the Ba'ath Turkmen to move against me—only because I had once stopped him to tell a joke about another Kurd teacher who was sick with sadness. The teacher was a gutless man who was trying to use the Ba'ath party thugs to permanently remove me from this world. The phony political charges were these:

I was preventing Kurd students from joining the Ba'ath Party.
I was persuading Kurdish students to attack Arab teachers.

God saved me, and Ba'ath officials assigned ne(mid-year) to another school—Imam Qasim High School. While there, I got the sad news that our Kurdish leader, Mullah Mustafa Barzani, had died, in America, on March 1, 1979. The news saddened millions of Kurds, but came as good news to Saddam and his Ba'ath party and other Kurd enemies. They began celebrating, shooting rifles into the air and expressing their happiness. That happiness, however, would not last.

Secrecy and fear abounded, and questions arose. Why had three prominent leaders died—Mullah Mustafa Barzani, the Shah of Iran, and Howary Bomedian (the Algerian president)? Maybe their deaths were related to the Kurdish 1975 revolution, and maybe certain people didn't want certain secrets revealed. I don't know.

In February of 1980, the same teachers who had urged the Ba'ath party to hang me persuaded a weak Kurdish teacher, Imam Qasim, to attack me with harsh words. I asked him to sit down with me and discuss his complaints. I wanted to reason with him, but he ran to the Ba'ath principal's room and obtained a sharp tool, which he intended to use against me. I wrested it away from him, however, and with it I made a cross mark on his back. I said, "Stop fighting, or I will insert this sharp tool into your heart." Thanks to God he stopped, and backed away. That teacher later became my best friend. I had awakened him. I had opened his eyes to the terrible events occurring in Kurdistan.

While I was dealing with the Ba'ath party's injustices and threats, Saddam, the vice president, was urging President Ahmad Hassan Albakir to attack Iran, a country that had refused to move against the Kurdish revolution. President Ahmad Hasan Albakir refused to do so, and Saddam had his son, Haytham, assassinated under the guise of a car accident. He then had President

Ahmad injected with poison, which killed him. Saddam took over, making himself the president of Iraq.

Iraq and the Iran war (1980-1988)

On September 22, 1980, as I was working as a math teacher and planning my future, Saddam launched a war against Iran, a conflict that killed off a future for many Iraqis and Iranians. The Ba'ath party forced me to stay at the school building day and night. I would go home for meals, but then was compelled to return to the empty school building. Saddam's Ba'athists wanted to keep certain educated people, including teachers, away from their houses, in order to keep them under firm Ba'ath control. The war was not in the Kurds' interest; it further oppressed Kurds. I began thinking about how my family could flee Iraq. But how? At this point, it was only a dream.

I tried to analyze and understand past events. Algeria's president died December 27, 1978. Mullah Mustafa died March 3, 1979. The Shah died July 27, 1980. Were there any connections? I was so confused. I listened to radio broadcasts, trying to learn more about Kurdistan's plight and troubles. My family and I were so afraid of the war, but we had no way to escape. Were we condemned to die from Iranians rockets? Or may be at the hands of Saddam's Ba'athist thugs, criminals all?

Tragedy in my family, June 1, 1981

I had five sons: Lukman, Yousif, Cameron, Saman, and the youngest son Rezgar. On June 1, 1981, my oldest son, Lukman (age 12) was hit and killed by a vehicle driven by an Arab Ba'athist, one of those that Saddam had resettled from the south in order to reduce the Kurdish influence in Kirkuk. My wife and I and our sons still grieve over this loss. But the tragedy strengthened my resolve to escape Saddam's brutal regime. But again, how?

In July of 1982, my family and I traveled to Turkey and Bulgaria to see if I could perhaps learn more about how to flee Iraq—and perhaps get to America. I met my Turkmen friend (Ghazi) in Istanbul. He was a childhood friend, the brother of Hasan Salih, who had been a student of mine. I taught him mathematics, and he ultimately became a professor at Istanbul University. Ghazi gave me some advice about how we might escape from Iraq, but I didn't know that he was in fact my enemy. I told him that since age fourteen I had wanted to go to America, but that it remained only a dream.

I had graduated from the University of Baghdad, and I sent my transcripts (from a Turkish post office) to a California university (UCLA), asking for admission. I never got a response, however, maybe because of the Saddam regime's censorship. I don't know. We came back from Turkey, and I put my house up for sale; and in June of 1983, I sold it for 50,000 Iraqi dinars. It was a very profitable sale.

I had a reason for selling: I wanted to be prepared to flee Iraq. Our nephews and nieces, however, revealed this secret ambition, and I began to fear severe retaliation at the hands of the Ba'ath party. All exits from Iraq had

126

been blocked, and we had no escape route. I rented a house, but I kept thinking about ways to get my family out of the country.

Saddam the killer, 1983

In 1983, Saddam gathered 8,000 innocent civilians from the Bazani tribe, none of whom were fighters, and put them in secret jails in the Iraqi desert, on the Iraq-Saudi Arabia border. His thugs then proceeded to kill them and bury them, hundreds each night. Saddam was an unbeliever, but God saw what he did.

Saddam also extended his dirty hands into high schools and colleges, and forced students to attend summer military camps. I was shocked when Ba'athists took my son Yousif and sent him to camps at Tazakormato and Sinjar, for training that lasted several months. He was only fourteen at the time. I had been thinking about ways to keep my sons away from Saddam's mandatory army system.

Unfortunately, Saddam again arranged a fake ceasefire with Jalal Talabani, and bloody conflict broke out between Masoud and Jalal Talabani Peshmergas (Kurdish freedom fighters). I was advising students from both sides—Jalal Talabani and Masoud Barzani followers. I was telling them that this bloody conflict was not right, and it was the enemy who was benefitting. It was so sad that a Kurdish hero, Faris Bawa, the brave Peshmerga had been assassinated in a cowardly way.

They had invited him to either lunch or dinner, and then opened up with machine gun fire and killed him.

While I was thinking about my sons and their welfare, I was also thinking about how I could protect myself from Ba'athists (Turkmen, Kurds, and Arabs) in Kirkuk. I applied to work in the Iraq parliamentary elections, thinking it would help me plan an escape. I knew the elections would be fraudulent, but my goal was to protect myself and my family from the Ba'ath henchmen, and to use election activity as some kind of a tool to aid my escape.

I informed the PUK through a student by the name of Abdulwahid what I was doing—that is, using parliament for protection and escape aid. The student was an honest and trustworthy individual from the village of Hama Soor, near Kirkuk. He would have been rewarded by the Saddam regime if he had given them my secret election plan. My witness for this dangerous plan was Dleir Khadir Omar (a PUK member in Kirkuk). I regret that I chose this election as a tool, since many Kurds did not understand why I was doing so.

After I failed in the election, I built my second house, in 1984. Many enemies in Ba'ath party did not understand why I was in the election. They did not know that I was waiting for an opportunity to flee Iraq.

Saddam and Chemical Ali

On March 16, 1988, Saddam and Chemical Ali bombarded the Kurdish city of Halabja with chemical weapons of mass destruction. They killed five thousand innocent civilians, and another fifteen thousand died gradually over a two-year period. Women continued to deliver disabled babies for several years. Also in 1988, in the Anfal campaign against Kurdistan, Saddam buried 300,000 Kurdish men, women, and children alive; and he destroyed 5,000 Kurdish villages in Iraqi Kurdistan, burning and bulldozing them.

As I watched the Kurdish tragedy unfold, and as we tried to deal with the pain over the loss of our son, I prayed to God, praying that He would help Kurds attain freedom—not just in Iraq, but also in Turkey, Iran, and Syria. I also developed a plan to get out of Saddam's education system, which was filled with violent individuals, men who especially hated Kurds. At that time, a teacher was expected to stay in his job for at least 25 years. Thus, I was unable to resign, since I had not completed the 25 years. My goal was to claim that I had health problems, then get out and develop an escape plan.

The Hero: Sheikh Ahmad Al- Jaber Al-Sabah
Saddam and Imam Khomeini signed a ceasefire agreement on August 20, 1988, ending the war between Iraq and Iran. Saddam and his regime did not believe they could survive a protracted war.

Although I was still saddened by Saddam's terrible Anfal campaign and the genocide in Halabja's, in

1988, I was cheered by a visit from a childhood friend, a Turkmen (WS) who visited Kirkuk following the 1989 ceasefire. He had come from America, and I was happy to see him. I visited him at his brother's house and gave him a live turkey, a gift that showed respect. The next day he agreed to take $2,100 of my money back to America, and to put in a bank for safekeeping, in the event I would visit America. He said, "I will give you a receipt to confirm that you gave me this money." I said, "No, I trust you." He left a few days later, and a month later I received a card from him showing a picture of "Chicago at Night." He wrote on the back that he had deposited the money.

Following the war, Saddam seemed to become even bolder and more arrogant, but I knew he was still a coward. He wanted to use Arab power to protect himself from Iran, and to deny Kurds their rights forever and ever. He set up a meeting in Baghdad with King Hussein, President Mubarak, the Prince of Kuwait, King Fahd, and Yemen President Ali Saleh. He asked them to form an Arab Union, a way for him to avoid repaying war loans to Kuwait and other Arab countries. He wanted to use oil money to make nuclear weapons, and thus increase his power.

The invited leaders agreed to Saddam's request, except for the Prince of Kuwait, who returned to Kuwait with a report. He knew that Saddam was spending Iraq's resources for weapons of war, not for his people, and Kuwait asked Saddam to repay the loan that he had received to fight the Iranians (1981-1988). Saddam then began distributing propaganda, accusing Kuwait of stealing Iraqi oil. Everyone knew, however, that this was a lie, since Kuwait had given Saddam billions of dollars to support his war machine. Saddam retaliated by halting all trade with Kuwait.

Ch. 13- Decision to Escape from Iraq to Turkey

Making a plan

The Halabja Kurdish atrocity, and the terrible Anfal campaign, and the loss of my oldest son all strengthened my resolve to flee Iraq, to turn dreams into reality. In May of 1989, I retired from teaching, after 23 years of service, two years before the normal 25 years. I had to plan this carefully, because my neck lay close to Saddam's knife. I claimed that I had to retire early for health reasons. The Ba'ath-Kurd principal at my school told the school district office that he thought I was feigning illness. I knew about his shameful relations with other Ba'ath educators, and I knew that he wanted me permanently out of the way. I carried out the fake illness plan for eight years.

Upon retirement, I sold my second house, which gave me a profit of about 10,000 Iraqi dinars. I went to live in my brother-in-law's house for one month, and then I rented a house in Raheem Awa, in Kirkuk, and began developing plans to flee the country

In July of 1989, I worked for a time as a civil engineer, for my brother, who had one-year temporary contract, and I earned thousands of dinars. With this money ($25,000 in U.S. dollars), I went into business with my childhood Turkmen friend, Ismael Haqqi, who owned a wall paint shop. He had revealed the plan to assassinate Mullah Mustafa in 1958, when we were onlyin sixth grade. He was half paralyzed, but he was

132

able to walk very slowly with the use of a cane, and he was able to talk.

While I was working at the paint shop, another Turkmen friend approached me and said, "Why did you give Ismael this huge amount of money!" I said, "Why do you want to know?" He said "Ismael is a big fraud maker person, and I'm afraid he will keep your money, and you will never see it again!" He added, "Ismael's high school diploma is a fake; he bought it in the city of Mosul, in 1965."

I learned more from this individual. I learned that the results of national tests given to students in their final year of high school had been interfered with. In June of 1964, the train that was carrying the Bakaloria test notebooks from Kirkuk to Baghdad was also transporting a "mafia" member of the education department, and he switched the covers on the test booklets. That is, he put the booklet covers of strong Kurd students on the booklets covers of weak Turkmen students. Thus, I lost my chance to attend the College of Architecture, and my brother, Musa, lost his chance to attend the Medical College in Baghdad.

I had always wondered what had happened to my scores, and now twenty-six years later I learned the truth; I learned the reason I had gotten such low test scores. After a few months at the paint shop, I asked Ismael to return my money. He said, "I do not have it now, but I will have it." And to my surprise he did return it, making my escape plan more possible. In July of 1990, after the engineering work and the paint shop work, I was able to obtain a business card and to engage in export and import activities. This allowed me to engage in certain business transactions, and to further develop plans to flee Iraq.

Taha and the Turkish businessman

On July 27, 1990, I traveled to Turkey with 30,000 dollars worth of goods, which I intended to sell them to Mamad Abi, a Turkish business man who resided at Sari Ali Suqaqi, Khadir Koy/Istanbul. My plan was to place my money somewhere in Turkey. Then later, when I was fleeing with my family through Turkey, I would reclaim it and use to get to America.

On this business trip, I arrived in Istanbul by bus, and went to the hotel my family had stayed at in 1982. The next day, in the presence of Ghazi, I called my friend (W.S.) in America and said, "I am in Turkey, please W.S., send my money to me, because I now need it. This request disturbed him. He said in an angry tone, "Your money was taken from me at the airport in Baghdad by police." I knew immediately that this was a lie, but I did not change my tone, and I calmly asked him about his family and how he was doing. I maintained a respectful attitude, and ended the conversation.

I turned to Ghazi and related the conversation. Ghazi was surprised, and said that W.S. had never told him anything about any kind of airport incident. He added, "W.S. stayed in Istanbul at my house for fifteen days. He had purchased a quantity of gold, and he seemed comfortable and at ease. He did not describe any unusual happening during his flight from Iraq to Turkey, and then to America. My friend W.S. had lied to me, and that lie saddened me.

I stayed in Istanbul for a few weeks, waiting to get my money from Mamad Abi, the Turkish businessman, but on August 2, 1990, Saddam invaded Kuwait, and Mamad Abi refused to pay me for the goods. When I would press him, he would say, "Those goods are short of business papers." He knew that I couldn't obtain any paperwork in Iraq—or even call. The Saddam regime had closed the borders and stopped all travelers from entering or leaving Iraq.

I had lost my money, and I returned to Kirkuk on August 15, 1990, in a sad state of mind. I knew that Mamad Abi was a thief and that his excuses for not paying me were false. I wondered how he could enjoy his life, knowing that he had stolen from me. I was sure that God would help me recover from that loss, but my escape plan had been disrupted. Nonetheless, with God's help I knew it would ultimately succeed.

The castaway Baath man and my family's future
On August 16, 1990, I arrived home in Kirkuk, and Malika (my wife) said to me, "Hide yourself and don't go out of the home."

I said, "Why?"

She said, "Ba'ath is looking for you. The Ba'ath wants to take you and two of our sons to Kuwait, to fight."

I was shocked. I had been thinking only about the way Mamad Abi had robbed me of money, and now I had to think about how to protect my family from the murderous Ba'ath party. Malika said, "Ba'ath yesterday captured one of our sons and jailed him in a bathroom at Ba'ath headquarters in Raheem Aawa. They wanted to find out if you were in Kirkuk or not. They did not believe us when we told them that you were in Turkey on business."

Early in the morning of the next day, I heard a hard knock on our main door. I opened it and stepped out, and saw immediately that the knock had been delivered by an Arab, a man from the Ba'ath party. He had come from the middle of Iraq, and not from Kirkuk. My wife and sons stayed huddled behind the main door, fearful and anxious. He asked me in a barbaric and loud voice, "Where were you yesterday?"

I said, "I was in Turkey on business for twenty days."

He said, "Show me your passport." I located my passport and showed it to him. He looked at it and said, "In one week, you and your two sons must join our Jaysh Sha'abee (Saddam's civilian Army), and you must join us in Kuwait to fight our enemy, America." He then left without saying another word. I knew that war was about

136

to break out between the coalition forces and Saddam's forces.

I feared for the safety of my sons, and I knew I had to find a way to flee Iraq. I traveled to Sulaymaniyah and met with Malika's cousin, Hama Siddeeq, to see if he could help me contact our freedom fighter leader, Fatih Shwani. But my cousin feared the Ba'ath party in Sulaymaniyah, and he would not let me see the Peshmerga, Fatih Shwani, whom I was hoping would help me escape. Hama Siddeeq had a right to be afraid, because the penalty for his assistance could have been death by hanging.

I returned to Kirkuk the next day feeling that there was no hope, and then a week later I called on m father's cousin, Ahmad Haji Arif, in Sulaymaniyah, but he too was fearful and would not help me. I refused to give up, however, and I called on my brother-in-law, Najim. He met with his shop partner, Hasan, and brought up the subject of a possible escape plan.

That same day the three of us traveled to the cities of Ranya and Qala Diza, on the border of Iran. Hasan was from that area, and he had found a young man, a small shop owner who had agreed to find a smuggler. My spirits rose. I thought that I might have found a smuggler who would help us escape Saddam's criminal system, but the young man said, "This escape to Iran is not guaranteed to succeed, since you will have a wife with you, and the escape convoy is frequently exposed to looting and theft" I looked at my brother-in-law, and he looked at his friend, and then both informed me that we would have go to back to Sulaymaniyah. I had failed again, and I returned to Kirkuk the next day, again in a sad state of mind.

After these several failed attempts to find a way out of Iraq, I decided to go to the city of Zakho, to discuss an escape plan with Waleed, another brother-In-law. He had been a teacher in Batova/ Zakho, a Kurdish village close to the Turkish border. We met at the home of Waleed's former student, Ayyoub, and his brother Salah, in Zakho. But neither one could help us; neither could refer us to a smuggler. So we returned to Kirkuk, a six-hour drive.

For the next two months, I continued to search for a way to flee, but could not find an escape path. Finally, a Turkmen friend, Khaldoon, directed me to another Turkmen, a man by the name of Hussein Salih, who Khaldoon said might be able to help me. I knew that this man could have informed the Saddam criminal system about my plan, and in so doing probably would have been rewarded. But he had been a childhood friend, and he had no intention of reporting me to the Ba'ath thugs.

Taha and his family flee Iraq
On October 25, 1990, following Khaldoon's instructions, I went to Hussein Salih's house. We had been neighbors for forty years, and I also knew his brothers, Ghazi and Dr. Hasan Salih, both of whom resided in Turkey, their second country. I told them what

I needed, and they agreed to help me. I said, "How much will it cost?"

He said, "For you it is free. I remember that your father took care of my father when he was dying; he read aloud the Quran to my father."

I said to myself, "Hussein Salih is faithful and trustworthy, and he knows that I taught his brother, Hasan Salih, math without charging him, so that he could pass the Iraqi National Test."

On November 3, 1990, the smuggler, Hussein Salih, and two other men, Ahmad Shatir Bazzaz and the leader of the smuggler Rasheed Agha, of a Kurdish tribe, came to my house to discuss a plan. I was surprised to see that each was carrying a handgun, and then I realized that all of them were working for the Ba'ath party.

My wife, Malika, prepared a special lunch, and I asked again about the cost of this dangerous operation. I thought it would be about 2,000 dinars, tops. One Iraqi dinar at the time was equivalent to three U.S. dollars. They said, "The price is 15,000 dinars." I was shocked. This was equivalent to 45,000 U.S. dollars in 1990. I knew, however, that I had to agree to their terms. They were members of the Ba'ath party, and now knew my plan, and I knew I had to pay.

The important thing was to save my family from the cruel and possibly deadly Saddam regime. I desperately wanted to keep my sons out of the upcoming Gulf War. I also knew that Saddam would be pushed out of Kuwait—and probably out of Iraq, too. Therefore, I agreed to pay the forty-five thousand, and told them I would pay when it came time to flee.

The smugglers left my home, and I called on my neighbor, who was a relative and an agent of my house's landlord. I told him that we were going to visit Baghdad and look for work, and I said that if by chance we did not return after a month, he had the right to rent the house to someone else. I also said that Hussein Salih, who was the landlord agent's friend, would ship our furniture to Baghdad and hand over the house key. The agent did not know that Hussein Salih was a smuggler.

What I said to my neighbor, about our going to Baghdad, was a white lie, but it was part of the plan that I thought would save our lives. The landlord was one of Saddam's security officer's relative. If he had learned about our escape plan, we would have surely been hanged.

I knew that our escape attempt would be complex—and highly dangerous. There were three possibilities:

Saddam's security and military people would arrest us at the Iraqi-Turkey border and then execute us.

If we didn't succeed in escaping, and Saddam's security people didn't find out about our attempt, we would have to return to our house and await God's mercy.

We could succeed. We might escape Iraq and get to Turkish territory. We would not return to our house, and after a month it would be rented out to someone else.

On November 8, 1990, my wife and I visited my mother, who was ill and half-paralyzed, and we kissed her hands. She was amazed—our visit was so sudden. I gave her $1200, a huge amount of money. The gift surprised her. I hugged her, and my eyes and my heart said the last goodbye, but I did not speak, and I did not weep. I did not tell her that we were planning to escape the next day. It was difficult to leave her house, because I knew I would never see her again—but I had to go.

My wife and I left—our hearts filled with pain. I was feeling that my mom had died the moment I left her. I knew that she would be waiting for our next visit, maybe in a day or two. But I knew that she would never see me again, and I felt like I, too, had died.

That evening my brother, Abbas, came to our house and told me that he was concerned about our safety. He feared that the Ba'ath thugs would kill us. He said that Hussein Salih's daughters had spread the news, in their girls' high school, that Taha and his family had escaped to Turkey.

I said, "How do you know that?"

He said, "My daughters are in the same school as the daughters of Hussein Salih."

I angrily denied that we were leaving and told him to "get out of our house." I wanted to preserve his safety. I didn't want him to know anything about our plan, in case the Ba'ath henchmen confronted him and asked him what he knew, or what he had known.

Ch. 14- Fleeing from Kirkuk to the USA

Preparing to escape

Early on the morning of November 9, 1990, we prepared to flee Iraq. I sent my three sons from Kirkuk to Hawler, a city that was also called Erbil, and a city in which my sister resided. Each son carried a small shoulder bag. It was a good day to leave. Evacuation exercises were being conducted in Kirkuk. People were moving from Kirkuk to Altoon Kopri, where tents had been pitched to receive them. With all the commotion, I knew we would not draw undue attention.

On that afternoon, the smugglers Hussein Salih and Ahmed drove a Super Toyota car to a spot near our house, and parked it. My wife, my youngest son, and I exited the house, but closed the curtains and left the lights on—to indicate to Saddam's security people that we were still in the house. My wife and I took seats in the back of the car, and we took off for Erbil, with Ahmad at the wheel. My wife, Malika, and I were very worried. We did not know what lay ahead. We only knew that we could no longer live under Saddam's brutal oppression.

After driving for an hour, and after passing three of Saddam's security checkpoints, we arrived in Erbil and went straight to my sister's house, where my three sons awaited us. I gave Hussein Salih and Ahmad the $45,000 fee they had demanded and a key to the rented house in Kirkuk.

My sister then prepared dinner. She knew that we were fleeing that very night, and she feared for us. But we did not tell her about our plans, and she did not ask about them. We wanted her to be able to deny any knowledge of our flight to Turkey. We did not want to endanger her life. We knew that Saddam's security forces would execute anybody involved in the escape

The two smugglers and I then drove to the head smuggler's house, a man by the name of Rasheed Agha, who seemed to develop a sad expression when he saw me with the two other smugglers. All three then conducted a conversation among themselves, but I could not understand what they were saying. A few minutes later, the smuggler Ahmad Bazzaz and I returned to my sister's house. Smuggler Hussein Salih stayed behind, in Rasheed Agha's house

Nightfall arrived, and Ahmad said, "It's time to go" My sister and my wife began to cry like babies, and my sister tried to hold us and to prevent us from leaving. She hugged us, and the tears in my eyes were killing me. We had made a plan. We agreed that upon our arrival in Turkey, the smuggler, Rasheed Agha, would give my teacher retirement identification to Hussein Salih. Then when Hussein Salih returned, he would give the document to my sister, providing proof that we had made it into Turkey.

My sister finally calmed down. We said goodbye to her and her family, but then she again began to cry. It was an emotionally painful moment for her. We left the house and stepped into the Toyota. The car was crowded, with seven people inside. My youngest son sat on my lap, and the other three sons occupied the back seat. As we tried to get comfortable, the driver made his way to a residential area in Erbil, where a Land Rover awaited us.

We exited the car, and I noticed that Hussein Salih and Rasheed Agha were conversing with two armed men. These two men placed our bags in the Land Rover, and told me that my son, Cameron, would ride in the front with Rasheed Agha, the driver. Malika and I would sit in the second seat with the one of the armed men. My other sons—Rezgar, Saman, and Yousif—would sit in the third seat with the second armed man. Hussein Salih and Ahmad then left in their Toyota, leaving us alone with Rasheed Agha and his two armed men.

Rasheed Agha was the leader. His chest was covered with belts of bullets, and he carried a machine gun, which he placed on the floor of the vehicle, on the passenger side. Both of his men also carried machine guns. They belonged to one of Saddam's Kurdish militias, and their military post was apparently near the Turkish border.

The entire family found a way to fit into the Land Rover, each carrying a small shoulder bag. The vehicle made its way out of Erbil, passing safely through the Iraqi security checkpoint. As the vehicle continued, I began to think about our last dinner with my sister and her family. I think it was a stew, a dish of rice and green beans and lamb. While dining, I was not thinking about food. My mind was totally focused on the escape—but I was also wondering if this might be our last meal. I knew that we were embarked on a dangerous and potentially deadly journey.

We sat silently in the vehicle; you could have heard a pin drop. The darkness surrounded us, illuminated only by the vehicle's headlights. I was so afraid for my family, and I knew they too were afraid. I kept looking at their innocent faces, wondering if we would survive, if we would make it out alive. We stayed silent and calm, even though I knew we had only about a twenty percent chance of surviving—not a fifty-fifty chance as in a coin toss game. Yes, I had made a bold decision, and I was aware of the dangers, but I knew we had no choice. We had to find a better life.

We headed toward the Turkish border, through Salahaddeen city, Shaqlawa city, and the Galee Ali Beck area. The vehicle passed safely through several Iraqi security checkpoints, and we arrived in Diana city, where we changed direction and headed toward Hasarost Mountain. The driver, Rasheed Agha, suddenly stopped the vehicle and said to us, "Everyone get out and take your bags." He then told two of my sons, Rezgar and Cameron, to stay in the vehicle with the leader, Rasheed Agha. This was part of the plan. We were close to one of Saddam's military posts, and there were 14,000 Iraqi soldiers in the area, and we had to split up. The vehicle then took off, leaving behind me, Malika, and two of our sons. It moved ahead to the final checkpoint, which was part of a huge military post.

Malika, two of my sons (Yousif and Saman), the two assistants with their machine guns, and I moved very cautiously to the rear of the military installation. We intended to walk for only twenty to thirty minutes. The cloudy night was pitch black, no moon or even stars. We were walking on dry leaves, which made noise, and we were breathing hard. Our hearts were beating like drums. The assistants told us, "Please walk quietly and slowly, because we are targets for the Iraqi soldiers."

Malika said, "Please, stop. I have no energy to go further, and I am going to die." She said a few times to us "I will stay behind and die. You all keep on going.

We all stopped, and Malika lay on her back and lost consciousness. I put my hands under her head, and very quietly said, "Please wake up and take deep breaths."

She awoke and asked me, "Taha, where are our sons?"

I said, "They are here, my dear." She began walking again, but a ray of military light passed over our heads, and we hit the ground. After a few minutes, we got up and resumed our trek, and we walked for more than an hour.

I asked the assistants, "Please, why are we late in joining our other two sons?"

They told me, "Sorry, Mr. Muhammad, we lost our way. We have not seen this area for more than four years." I had fallen and cracked my eye glasses, but I had avoided some danger. I had come close to falling into a deep valley. We climbed a dusty hill, going up two steps and then sliding down one step.

We waited for two hours, the agreed upon waiting time. Suddenly we heard the sound of a machine gun. We thought at first that we were the targets, but after we saw that we were safe, we had another thought. We wondered if maybe our other two sons, Cameron and Rezgar, and Rasheed Agha, had been killed, as they tried to pass through one of Saddam's military checkpoints.

Family members united on November 10, 1990
We kept on going, feeling as though God had given us some super powers, some extra strength that allowed us to move quickly and to join my two sons. We knew our lives were in danger, but we stayed strong, and we finally reached the top of a hill—and then our nightmare ended. We saw the Land Rover, and our two sons, and Rasheed Agha. We were ecstatic. We could not stop hugging one another.

We had made it through the most dangerous checkpoint in the world. We had made it through the valley of death. Perhaps God was watching over us on that dark night, or maybe He just answered our prayers. I think often about that night, and I remember it as "the night of many miracles."

We got into the vehicle, and I saw that Rasheed was angry. He thought we had taken too long to arrive. The plan was that he would wait for thirty minutes, but it had taken three hours to reach him. My son, Cam, told me later that Rasheed had wanted to proceed, that he was prepared to leave us behind, thinking that we had either been killed or captured.

We felt momentarily happy. We had escaped the clutches of the brutal Saddam. We all got into the vehicle again and continued our dangerous journey. I said to myself, "If we had fled Iraq in 1980, then my oldest son could have been with us." I cried silently, but it was dark, and no one could see my tears. I was weeping over the memory of my oldest son, a fine boy who had been run over and killed by one of Saddam's Arab mercenaries, in Kirkuk in 1981.

As we came down a long, steep hill, a herd of wild pigs ran toward our vehicle. Our leader, Rasheed Agha, stopped the vehicle, and began firing his weapon over the pigs' heads, trying to make them change direction. I begged him, "Please stop shooting. Saddam's soldiers will see us and shoot us." He replied, "These pigs are more dangerous than Saddam's soldiers." The pigs disappeared, and we continued on, arriving at a shallow river. We washed our dusty faces, and drank from this quiet stream, one that ran down from the mountains.

We resumed our journey, crossing the 100-meter-wide river in our vehicle. We went up a high hill, and then down, and then smuggler Rasheed Agha stopped the vehicle. I was surprised. He turned to me and said, "You did not pay enough for this trip."

I said, "I paid Hussein Salih and Ahmad the entire cost."

He replied, "No, you have to pay me, too."

I knew the family was in a dangerous situation, surrounded by dangerous Ba'ath party men, who were carrying machine guns. Even though they were Kurds, they had sold themselves out to Saddam's party. My wife hit the side of my chest with her elbow and said, "Take this gold coin and give it to him."

Rasheed Agha took the coin and said, "This is not enough."

Malika gave me a second gold coin, and Rasheed continued to say it was not enough. He finally took a total of six gold coins from us. They had been fastened to a necklace around Malika's neck, seven in all. We retained only one coin. Rasheed Aghahad used machine gun power to steal our gold coins. He had sacrificed his dignity and betrayed his religion and his Kurdish faith.

We slid down to the edge of another river on the Iraq-Turkey border. I told my sons, "We will transfer our eight shoulder bags from this side of the river to the other side."

The thief Rasheed Agha said "No, my assistants will bring your bags to the other side of the river." He also said, "Early in the morning, after some rest this night among the trees in the forest, you must go to that building on the mountain in Turkey and ask them to take you to Istanbul. Then they will help you get to America."

Crossing the river from Iraq to Turkey: November 10, 1990

We started to cross the river, but the current was strong, and the water was very cold. It was snow water that was coming down from Karlikol Deresi (Ice Lake Valley). The river bottom was bumpy and treacherous, and filled with slippery, sharp rocks. We had to fight the water, and in the darkness Malika slipped and fell, and dropped her purse, which drifted away. But the smuggler, Ismail, and my son, Saman, were close to her and they grabbed her and stabilized her. Saman stayed close to her until they reached the Turkish shore. I was still in the river, helping my youngest son, Rezger. Only I and one of my sons knew how to swim.

Suddenly, while we are still in the middle of the river, we heard the sound of machine guns, and we hid ourselves in the water for a short time. The shots, however, were not being fired in our direction. We were temporarily safe, but we knew we were still in danger. We still had to fear soldiers from Iraq, Iran, and

Turkey—countries that had tried, and were still trying, to put down Kurdish rebellions.

We made it to the other side of the river, but then faced another obstacle. The bank was overgrown with hundreds of thorn trees and bushes that blocked our way. I tried to make a safe gate through the thorns, but it was impossible. Finally, I painfully dragged myself along on my stomach and made a path, and my family members followed. At last we were in the Kurdish part of Turkey. We sat for a time in the mud, shivering and worried. We feared that Turkish soldiers might think we were Kurdish Peshmergas and begin shooting at us.

My youngest son, Rezgar, was eleven at the time, and he could not stop crying, and I could not help him. Saman, my third son, stayed active, rubbing the shoulders of his brothers, Yousif and Camron, which helped relieve the cold and cramping. The chill had entered deep into our bones, and fear had entered deep into our hearts. We waited two hours for the dawn, waiting to see each other and see the path ahead. I was sad, but at the same time we were silently laughing. We resembled chickens who had been thrown into the river.

Malika had lost her shoes in the river, as had my youngest son, who had also cut his foot on a rock. Our bodies were still shaking from the cold, but fortunately the smuggler's assistants had brought all our bags to us from the Iraqi side river—all except one, and it was an important one. It contained my college certificate, marriage certificate, medicines, and four passports, all of which had been stamped with visas by the Turkish embassy in Baghdad three months earlier, in July of 1990.

Rasheed Agha: unfaithful to Kurd refugees

Rasheed Agha had learned which bag was most important. He had heard the ungrateful smuggler, Hussein Salih, say to me in Kirkuk, "Don't put your passports, money, or gold in your pocket, because officials at the checkpoints in Iraq might detain you and confiscate your valuable items." He said, "Put all important items into one bag, and let that bag stay under your feet in the vehicle." I trusted the smuggler, Hussein Salih, and I followed his advice, but I did keep my money and gold in my pocket. I did not bring any Iraqi money. I had changed my money to gold. I had only about $350 in my wallet. I trusted the smuggler, Hussein Salih, because I thought he was grateful. He had told me in Kirkuk, "I remember how your father took care of my father when he was dying."

I realized at 3:30 a.m. that the smuggler Rasheed Agha had taken my important bag; I went down to the river and demanded that he return it, but the smugglers disappeared as quickly as a magic lamp's demon. I came back to our muddy spot among the bushes and saw that my youngest son, Rezgar, was still in a lot of pain. He had not slept the entire night.

We sat quietly, fearing that Turkish soldiers might shoot us. They were around the Iraq border, ready to kill any Kurdish peshmergas, and they were a danger.

The sun sent its first rays around 5:00 a.m., and we got to our feet and prepared to find a Turkish military office, to inform officials that we were going to America.

Let me tell you my feelings. Imagine that there is only one step between you and death. How would that make you feel? That is how I felt in those nighttime hours, as we struggled to survive. The only thing that kept us going was a thing called hope, hope that all our struggles would lead us to a safe path—and we would be free. We would live in peace. It is a terrible thing to live in an endless state of fear, fearing that any moment could be your last, fearing that you might lose your loved ones.

We stayed strong that dark night. We were determined to follow our dream, to look forward, not backward. We kept saying to ourselves, "We can do this. We can keep going, and we can overcome this challenge and reach freedom." We had passed through an area in Iraqi Kurdistan that contained 14,000 of Saddam's soldiers and thousands of land mines.

There were no civilians in that area, because Saddam had destroyed 5,000 of our Kurds and their villages during the Anfal military operation of 1988. Yes, we passed through an area that contained wolves, dogs, wild pigs. We had crossed a cold and wild river, and we would ultimately reach a land of freedom—the United States of America.

Ch. 15- Taha and His Family in Turkey

Turkey's border military barracks

Dawn arrived, and although we were still being tormented by bitter cold and the loss of my college certificate at the hands of the thief Rasheed Agha, we welcomed the sun, and we wanted to keep walking. My son Rezgar, however, was still suffering from the cold and the intense pain in his feet, and he could not stop crying. Walking for him was difficult, so my oldest son, Yousif, put him on his back, and we started walking up the mountain to the Turkish military base.

Turkish military barracks on the border of Iraq

We formed a single line and found a path that led to the Turkish military office. As we walked along, we suddenly spotted a line of Turkish soldiers coming down the mountain on another path. I yelled at them, "Hey, we are refugees from Iraq; we have come to Turkey seeking help, I am a teacher, and my family is with me."

They aimed their machine guns at us, and ordered us to raise our arms, and then approached, guns aimed directly at our chests. We were alarmed, to say the least, and then the dogs approached us and began sniffing, while the soldiers searched our pockets and shoulder bags. Thanks to God, we had no weapons. They put us in their line, and we began walking, bedraggled refugees with muddy and wet clothes. We reached the mountain top, and when the guard at the entrance to the military post saw us, he began shaking his head back and

155

forth, signaling (I thought) that we were headed for trouble.

We entered the base, and soldiers pushed us into a small jail-room, but we welcomed the warmth of the fireplace and the opportunity to dry our clothes and ourselves. Soldiers gave us bread, cheese, and tea; and they served us a lunch. We were happy and looking forward to good news, to news that we would be moved to Ankara, Turkey, and then would fly to America, as the Turkmen smuggler, Hussein Salih, had told us, when we were still in Kirkuk.

Tonight the entire family will die

That evening, two officers entered our jail-room, and we were glad to see them. We thought they had to come to welcome us and to let us know when we would be going to Ankara, to meet United Nations officials. We got to our feet, showing respect, but one official ordered us to sit down, and our happiness quickly turned to terrible fear. He said, "Tonight we will hand you over to Iraqi soldiers." We were shocked, and immediately recalled the following true story.

A month before our escape, Saddam's army people had captured a Turkmen family who had been smuggled from Iraq into Turkey. Soldiers killed the father and boys at the Iraq-Turkish border and handed over the mother to Kirkuk security forces. Criminals in those forces tore off her clothes, and they brought her father in, to see her in this state. A few days later her father died: he was overcome by the shame of it all.

156

I told the officer that I had paid a smuggler $45,000 and that I had lost my property, and I said, "And now you want to hand us over to Saddam? Do you know what will happen to us?"

He said "Yes, you all will die"

I said, "I knew Iraq was a dangerous place for us, but I thought that Turkey would protect us."

He said, "We can't help you. Prepare to die."

My wife began to cry and to plead for some mercy, but they would not listen. They pushed us out of the jail cell and onto the front yard of the building. A Turkish flag went up, and sad military music began to play.

I said to a soldier, "What is going on?"

He said, "You are all going to die tonight, and this is part of the ceremony marking your death."

Malika, who was standing beside, fainted. My sons stayed strong and did not cry out, but tears streamed down their cheeks. We were shocked. We never expected this from the Turks. Otherwise we would have gone to Iran, which perhaps would have been better. It was clear that Saddam and Turkish officials had agreed to this plan, to kill refugees. But why? Why would Turkey help Saddam, America's enemy? My sons were

157

looking at me, but I could only look away. I had given them a death sentence. I looked at the sky and thought that maybe I would see the God that created us—and that He would rescue us, so that we could continue our lives in America.

Gold coin to the Turkish officer, November 10, 1990

While I was silently pleading for God's help, Malika got back to her feet and quietly told me to give a gold coin to the officer. I located the biggest gold coin we had, and I said to the officer, "This is a gift from my wife to your wife."

He said, "I am not married yet, but I have a fiancée."

I said to him. "OK, it is a gift to your fiancée!"

He replied, "I will take it later."

I returned to Malika's side and informed her about what had transpired. In seconds, we found ourselves sitting in the back of a military truck, looking like cows about to be butchered. We were going back to the Iraq border, where we would be turned over to Saddam's people, and they would presumably collect their bonuses. Who knows, I thought, maybe the smuggler (Hussein Salih) and robber (Rasheed Agha) would also get some kind of bonus. Why else would they have directed us to come into this situation?

Begijny village on Turkish side

We arrived that night at a village called Begijny. We approached the gate of a house, and I gazed up at the sky, looking for God, but all I could see were stars, covered with our blood. We stepped down from the truck and entered the house of the village headman, Hussein Beck. The civilian gunmen and soldiers were waiting outside. The convoy officer ordered the village headman to turn us over to the Iraqi military forces at midnight.

The officer I had spoken to earlier turned and began leaving the large living room. I followed him and stopped him, and placed the gold coin in his right hand, which he dropped into his pocket. I suddenly felt a ray of hope, but I was still fearful and uncertain. I returned to the living room and informed my wife about what I had done. The officer came back to the room and told the village leader that he would return at 9:00 p.m. The officer then rejoined his people and returned to the Turkish military base.

The Kurdish family at the Beck house prepared an excellent meal for us, but we were unable to eat. We knew we were about to die. They insisted that we eat; it was part of their culture, and we managed to consume a tablespoon of vegetable soup. All the village people, Kurds, came to the house and expressed sympathy for our plight. They wanted to find a way to save us, but they were powerless.

A few hours passed, and then the Turkish military officer whom I had bribed returned and told the village leader to keep us in his house for three days. It was good news. We felt that we had a temporary reprieve and that we would not die that night, but we knew that we were not free—and that our lives could end in three days.

Uncle Madani the hero of Kurdistan in Turkey, November 17, 1990

Three days passed, and Hussein's uncle, Madani, appeared and took us to the village of Sebete, twenty kilometers away from the Iraq border. We moved into his big house, with his big family, and they treated us in a very respectful fashion. Seven days passed, and on the seventh day Madani came to us and said, "Run into a valley and hide yourselves there immediately." I asked him why. He said, "Turkish soldiers are near my village, so go all of you and hide." We ran into a valley that was dense with trees and that contained a small pond. We stayed only a few hours. Madani found us, and we returned to his house. The Turkish soldiers had left the village.

Madani then told me that he had a relative in Semdinli city by the name of Jalal Beck. He was a well known and wealthy merchant, and Madani thought he might be able to help us contact Semdinli's governor, who might give us permission to become legal refugees.

Madani left, to go to Semdinli and to make contact with his relative, but unfortunately another Iraqi refugee family arrived and was staying in uncle Miran's house. This family consisted of Ahmad (husband), Samira (wife), Hanah (two-year old daughter), and

160

Qasim (single man, Ahmad's relative). This family persuaded me to leave Sebete. It was too close to Iraq, they said, and Turkish soldiers could still find us and hand us over to Saddam.

Criminal plan against my family

On November 22, 1990, I met Mullah Khan, a businessman in the import-export business who conducted business along the Turkey, Iran, and Iraq borders. He had come from Semdinli city to visit uncle Miran, a relative. He knew about our difficulties in Sebete, and he offered to shelter both families in his house, until we could become declared refugees in Semdinli. Ahmad and Qasim put together a plan. We would go to Semdinli city, which I agreed to, since Malika was sick and needed to see a doctor. Once there we would contact Jalal Beck for help in obtaining legal refugee status.

On November 24, early in the morning, Malika, Samira, and the baby Hanah left Sebete with truck driver Nasir, uncle Miran's brother. They were headed to Mullah Abdulla Khan's house in Semdinli. Khan's wife was from Erbil, Iraq, and I was sure that she would take care of Malika, Samira, and Hanah at her house.

The plan was for the truck driver, Nasir, to return to Sebete after eight hours, and then to take all of us to Semdinli, to Khan's house. We waited for Nasir outside Sebete. Night came, but Nasir did not come. I became very worried. I knew that Ahmad and Qasim had conspired against my family. I thanked God that four male relatives of the farmer whose house we were staying in came from Semdinli, and that they knew Mullah Abdulla Khan and the driver, Nasir. I shared with them my concern about Malika, and they promised to help me contact her the next day. I waited anxiously throughout the long night.

My youngest son, Rezgar age eleven travels alone

The new day came. The night had been a nightmare for me; I had not slept. I asked the four visitors the next morning to take my youngest son, Rezgar, who was eleven at the time, to his mom in Semdinli city, and they agreed to do so. It was a four-hour drive.

Looking back, I see that it was a big mistake to send my wife to Semdinli, and then the next day to send my son. They had become separated from the rest of the family, and we had no way of contacting them, although we knew the names of two families in Semdinli. It was also possible that my son would not be able to find his mom. Each day I waited anxiously for word from my wife and youngest son, but no word came. I asked myself, "What can I do?" I felt helpless, like a man who had lost both arms and legs. I couldn't think of any possible options.

One week later, I received a letter from Malika, informing me that she had Rezgar, but that she was unable to see a doctor, since she lacked a Turkish ID card. As I read the letter, I began to shiver with joy, knowing that my wife and son were safe, and that I still had my other three sons with me, in Sebete village.

A meeting in Sebete village

I met with the Ahmed, Qasim, and my three sons—Yousif, Camron, and Saman—and I told them, "I am going secretly to Semdinli by car to gain legal refugee status." I said to Ahmad and Qasim, "Please, while I am away, would you take care of my three sons?"

They said, "Yes, we will take care of your sons."

My sons and I then met at another spot in the village, and I said to them, "I think Ahmad and Qasim are bad men. If you see that they disappear from this village after my trip to Semdinli, this proves that they are criminals." I told my son, Cameron, "If these two men disappear from here, then you must go to Semdinli and take care of your mom."

Cameron said, "You will be there with Mom?"

I said, "Who knows if I will arrive there!"

My words seemed to sadden Cameron, but he promised to watch Ahmad and Qasim in Sebete village, and he said that he would take care of his mom in Semdinli city. I was worried about Malika, because I had inadvertently revealed to Ahmad that Malika was holding gold worth $25,000, half the profit from the house I had sold in Kirkuk. I thought that Ahmad might take that gold from Malika while she was alone with him. So I had sent my son, Rezgar, to protect her.

Taha's trip to Semdinli

On November 29, early in the morning, while standing at the edge of the dusty road that goes from Sebete village to Semdinli, a big unloaded truck stopped to give me ride. The driver's name was Shaheen, and when we began conversing he realized that I was not a Turk. I told him I had three sons in Sebete village and that I was going to Semdinli to see my wife and the youngest son—and to try and obtain legal refugee status. He said, "Your family is in three parts-- you on the road, your three sons in Sebete village, and your wife and youngest son in Semdinli!"

He seemed to sympathize with my situation, and he asked me, "Do you have someone to take care of your three sons in Sebete?"

I said, "Yes, the good hero man named Madani and his entire family are taking care of my sons."

Shaheen asked, "Where are your wife and youngest son staying in Semdinli?"

I said, "They are at Abdulla Khan's house, and his wife from Erbil, Iraq, is taking care of them"

He said, "Who is Abdulla Khan?"

I informed him that Abdulla Khan was the relative of Jalal Beck in Semdinli. He seemed relieved and told me not to worry about my wife and son. Jalal Beck is a very good person, he said, and not just famous in Semdinli, but famous all over Turkey. He said he would take me to Jalal Beck's house.

After twenty minutes of driving and conversing, he pulled off the main road and headed down a secondary road. After a five-minute drive, he stopped the truck and we joined a group of truck drivers who were barbequing a lamb and making tea over a wood fire. The other drivers asked about me, and Shaheen described my situation. One of the drivers then went to his truck and brought back a blue, oily, second-driver's set of clothes. He said to me, "Because you have no Turkish ID, it would be best to put away your teacher's clothes and put on these clothes. It will help you safely pass the Turkish checkpoints." I thanked him and immediately changed my clothes.

It was still morning, and I was hungry, and the drivers offered me some of their lamb. Shaheen and I finished our breakfast with them and continued on to Semdinli. We easily passed four or five checkpoints. At each checkpoint Shaheen would greet the soldiers, talk to them, give them Iranian apples, and keep them busy, so that they would not focus on me.

I stayed busy too, using some screwdrivers and pretending that I was a second driver working on the truck. Back on the road, Shaheen said, "There is a

165

refugee camp in my city of Wan, and it has at least fifty Iraqi refugees."

I asked him, "Are you sure?"

He said, "Yes, I saw that refugee camp on Turkish television."

I said, "Please, would you help me get to the Wan refugee camp? Please, but first I have to see my wife and youngest son in Semdinli." He promised to help me.

We neared the final checkpoint, in the middle of Semdinli city, and Shaheen stopped the truck and said, "Get out of the truck and begin walking across this farmland. I will pick you up after I pass the dangerous checkpoint." I walked about a mile through the muddy farmland. The heavy muddy shoes were tiring me, but that good man, Shaheen, was waiting for me.

We reached Semdinli city in late afternoon and found Jalal Beck's house. We both met with Beck, and he advised me that Van city might possibly accept refugees. He told his son to transport me (in his Mercedes car) back to Abdullah Khan's house, to rejoin Malika and son Rezgar. Shaheen said to me, "I will wait for you at the teashop." He gave Jalal Beck's son the name of a certain teashop and told him to drop me off there—after I had met with my wife and son at Abdullah Khan's house.

Malika, Rezgar, and I meet in Semdinli City

On November 29, at around 6:00 p.m., Jalal Beck's son dropped me off at Abdullah Khan's house. I was thrilled at the prospect of seeing my wife and son. I knocked on the door, and I heard my son yell, "My father is here!" He yelled the same words several times, and my wife came running to me. I almost thought she might injure herself.

They both hugged me, and tears rolled down my cheeks. Malika asked about our other three sons. She didn't like my dark-blue, oily driver's clothes; and she asked me why I was not wearing my teacher's suit. I began to describe the events of the day, but cut short my account, when I saw neighborhood kids gathering around us. I was afraid that they might report us to the Semdinli police.

Jalal Beck's son was still with me, and Mullah Khan's wife offered us tea. I said to Malika, "I am going now to Van city, which is five hours away by truck, and I am going to register myself in the refugee camp over there." My wife felt sorry for me. I had not shaved my beard since November 9, and I was still wearing the oily trucker clothes.

She was worried and said, "Our family has become three parts. I am far away from you by five hours, I am far away from our three sons by four hours, and you are far away from your three sons in Sebete village by nine hours, and in a foreign country!"

167

I replied, "I know Mullah Khan's phone number, and I will call you and update you about my situation. Please, don't leave this house." She began to cry, but I had no choice. I had to go to Van City. Jalal Beck's great son then drove me to the teashop, but came in with me to make sure that Shaheen would continue to transport me. Shaheen and I had tea, and then left for Van at 7:00 p.m. My heart was filled with pain, as I thought about my wife and sons and what they were enduring.

Mr. Muhammad on road to Van (Wan) city
The dark and cloudy sky further darkened my mood, but Shaheen drove on quietly, neither of us speaking. I was afraid of road thieves, police, soldiers— and I also feared the uncertain future that lay ahead. The hours went by, and I suddenly saw a flashing red light behind us. I said to myself, "That's it. I am trapped. This is the end of this dangerous trip for me. What can I do? What will my wife and sons do after I am killed on this dark and foreign road? Who will tell them about my death?" Then I thought, "No, death was at the border of Iraq, and God saved us. Now I am deep into Turkey. I will be safe."

Shaheen didn't tell me what the flashing light meant. He simply stopped the truck, and I was surprised to see a farmer with a herd of cows—and so late at night. Shaheen and I got down from the truck, surveyed the area, and then moved his truck to a small rise, where he began loading the cows. The farmer and I and Shaheen then got into the truck. I had not showered for a month, and the farmer had probably not showered for some time, and foul odors permeated the truck.

We continued on toward Van, when suddenly a strong light behind us signaled to Shaheen that he must pull over. He stopped and said to me, "Keep yourself hidden in the truck and stay calm." Shaheen and the farmer got down from the truck and went to the back, where they waited on the shoulder of the road. A policeman on a motorcycle drove up. He had been the source of the light. A loud argument ensued, but the voices quieted down after Shaheen and the farmer gave the policeman bribe money.

We again got on the road, moving toward Van, and I thanked God that the policeman had not seen me. Shaheen said to the farmer, "You put me in a difficult situation by not having health papers for the cows." The farmer said that he was sorry, and that next time he would bring the papers.

Van City, November 30

We reached Van at 1:30 a.m. and dropped off the farmer and his cows at the city's cattle market. Shaheen said to me, "I will drop you off on a street that is a half-mile away from the building that serves as a hotel for refugees. It is managed by the police"

I immediately changed into my teacher's suit, now dusty and dirty, and took out a gold coin. I said to Shaheen, "From this gold take out your driving cost."

He looked at me, and I could see that his eyes were filled with tears. He shook my hand and said, "Put your gold back in your pocket. I will pray that you reach your goal after this dangerous trip, but please don't mention my name to the police"

I began walking toward the hotel, the temporary refugee camp. I was both excited and nervous, and I asked God for help in reuniting my family. A drunken man tried to stop me, but I moved on and entered the hotel, and approached the receptionist, a policeman. I said, "Hello, I am an Iraqi refugee," and I placed my family's Iraqi birth identification on the table. I then got a rude reception.

A policeman took me out of the hotel, and two or three others began kicking me. I wanted to retaliate, but I did not respond. I knew that my first responsibility was to my family, and I had to stay calm. The police called their main office, and security people showed up, and pushed me into a police van. They did not return my family's Iraqi birth identification, and I was not able to ask them to return it. It had been turned over to other policemen.

They even took the card "Chicago at Night, which W.S. had mailed me. It was proof that W.S. had successfully gotten my $2,100 to America. As for my Iraqi identification papers, I was sure that the police would sell them. The policemen's loud voices and the vehicle noise sounded like a hundred fighters in battle.

Taha in jail in Wan city

The van passed through a crowd of people and finally stopped in front of an ugly building; it was the police station. A gentleman came out and said to me, "You are our guest tonight, and we will give you a nice dinner and a place to stay at an excellent hotel." I believed that damned gentleman, but then a civilian security fellow pushed me into a small room and closed the door, and I realized that I was in a jail.

An hour passed, and the door opened, and the police kicked a young Kurdish man into the room. He started asking me questions, and I began to think that he was a spy. I said to him, "I am a Kurd, a math teacher from Iraq, and I came here to get help. I want to get refugee status and get to America. Please stop asking me questions, because I am not Turkey's enemy."

A few more hours passed, and the police finally removed the young man from my jail cell. Morning had come, and I asked the shift officer, "Please, let me go to the bathroom, because I need to pray in the morning." He allowed me to leave the room, and I prayed, and then said to him, "I am so hungry. Would you please order two servings of shish-kabobs for you and me? Here is twenty dollars." He took the money and ordered kabobs. He allowed me to eat with him in his office, and then ordered police to return me to the jail-room.

On November 30, at 8:00 a.m. five security people came and removed me from the jail. They put me in a vehicle and drove to a dark and ugly security

171

building. One officer began asking me questions, and from time to time he would raise his hand, as though he were about to slap me. A second officer explained to him that I was elderly and had been a teacher, and that seemed to stop the threats.

I told the man my story, and told him that my three sons were waiting for me in Sebete village, and that my wife with our youngest son was was waiting for me in a house in Semdinli city, a house with a phone. He threatened again to slap me, but another officer stopped him, telling him that I was an educated man who had left Iraq with his family in order to find freedom—and that I was not a criminal. I had not come to Turkey to commit crimes.

I was later offered tea, but I was feeling sad, and I refused it. They drove me back to the police station, and forced me to go to a gold shop and exchange my last gold coin for Turkish money, for lira. The Turkish civilian security officer then made me buy a round-trip bus ticket for him and a one-way ticket for me—a ticket that would take me to another city and another place, the Hakkari city jail.

Taha escorted by security Turkish officer from Van city to Hakkari city

On November 30, at 3:00 p.m., the bus started out for Hakkari. All the Kurdish people in the bus were closely observing me. I understood their Kurdish Kirmanj language, so I knew they were talking about me. Several of them had been present when the police had captured me.

After a three to four-hour drive, we arrived at the Hakkari security building, where the Van security officer delivered me to the Hakkari security officer, who treated me well. He took me to dinner at the police dining hall. The next morning, he took my fingerprints, and began asking hundreds of questions, all of which I answered honestly. I did not avoid any of the questions. They then made me rent a taxi,and using my money, transferred me to the Semdinli jail.

Taha escorted from Hakkari to Semdinli police station

On December 1, I found myself in a taxi with a civilian police officer and another Kurdish gentleman, the individual the police in Semdinli had shoved into my jail-room to spy on me. He, too, had asked me questions, and I had answered them honestly. I had told him about my goal, to reach America. He spent only one night with me in that jail, but I think I taught him a lot about Kurds, and the Kurdish leaders: Mullah Mustafa, Jalal Talabani, Masud Barzani, Sheikh Mahmoud, Salahaddin Ayoubi, and others. I told him that we should not act like the beautiful Kurdish bird called "Kaww." I said that we have to help each other, regardless of political party.

The next day I was removed from the jail cell and placed on a chair at the police station, to wait for the police to process the paperwork. Suddenly, who should appear but my wife, my two sons, Cameron and Rezgar, and the refugees Ahmad, Qasim, Samira, and little Hanah. I had given my wife and son's address to the police in Van, so that we could possibly be reunited, and the police had arrested them. I was so happy to see my wife and two sons.

After many hugs and kisses, I asked my wife about our other two sons. She told me that they were in Sebete village, at hero Madany's house. We asked the police for help in bringing them from Sebete to this jail, a four-hour drive. But the police said they had no connection with that village. We were so worried; we had lost our connection to Sebete. I asked Malika about her escape to Semdinli, and she gave me the story.

These are her words:
:

Samira, the baby Hana, and I got into the truck with the driver, Nasser. When it started to move, I became frightened. None of my family members were present, and I did not have any Iraqi or Turkish identification papers. I wondered what would happen if Turkish police arrested me. The thought of it made me feel like my body was on fire. My heart seemed to speed up, and my breathing became rapid. I thought I might die of a heart attack.

While I was having all these thoughts, I saw that we were approaching a Turkish military checkpoint. The driver stopped, and a Turkish soldier came to the passenger side of the truck and looked at me strangely. I was frightened, and my face turned red from fear and shyness. The soldier went to the other side of the truck and said to the driver, "Who is this woman?" The driver said, "She is my sister, and she is going to the doctor. It is an urgent situation."

The soldier didn't seem to believe the story, but he was a merciful man. He could have taken me to jail, since I had no Turkish ID, but he waved us through the checkpoint. As the truck began to move, my heart began to beat normally. Samira looked at me; he was worried about me. Both of us, and the kid Hanah, were headed toward an unknown future.

After an hour of driving, Nasir stopped near a huge tree, close to a Kurdish village. He told us to stay here and that he would return in one hour. Samira, Hanah, and I waited until evening, but he did not return, and we were frightened. But a few Kurdish village women had found us, and they understood our situation. They gave us fresh grape, and water. We decided to go back to Sebete village, but we didn't know how to get there. The women told us we could rest at their houses, but we told them that if we left our spot, the truck driver would lose contact with us; therefore, we needed to stay.

Nasir finally returned. We scolded him for being late, and we were crying. He said, "I am sorry. I was collecting bushes to sell in Semdinli. It is safer for you at night because the Turkish soldiers will not recognize you as Iraqis." We then left, as the wonderful women and kids, who were so helpful, waved at us. We passed all the checkpoints safely, and we arrived in Semdinli, at

175

night. The driver stopped away from a house and told us to knock on the door. It was Mullah Abdulla Khan's house; and Samira, the baby Hana, and I got out of the truck and approached the house.

We walked over mud, snow and rocks, and we finally reached the door. Samira knocked, and a woman answered. She was surprised. We asked her, "Are you Mullah Abdulla Khan's wife?"

She said, "Yes, but who are you women?"

We told her our story and how Mullah Khan had given us permission to come to his house. She warmly welcomed us in. Mullah Khan's mother and kids all woke up from their sleep and welcomed us.

The next day, Rezgar arrived and was trying to find us. He passed in front of Mullah Khan's house, but he did not know that I was inside. Thank goodness, Samira called out loudly, "Rezgar. Rezgar."

I said, "Why are you yelling his name? Rezgar is in Sebete with his father."

She said, "No, he is here, and I am seeing him through the window, and he is moving away from the house." I ran out of the house. Yes, it was Rezgar! I started crying and thanking God that Rezgar had found us. He did not know Mullah Khan's house address.

Cameron escapes Sebete village alone

I asked Malika about our son, Cameron, and how he got to Semdinli. She told me the following story.

Again, these are her words:

Ahmad and Qasim first came from Sebete to Semdinli, without the knowledge of our sons. They came to Mullah Khan's door, but Mullah Khan's wife did not allow them to come in, because I had told her that they couldn't stay in this house. She sent them to Jalal Beck's house, the rich good man, in Semdinli. Before they left, they asked me to give them a piece of gold to pay a smuggler who had helped them get from Sebete village to Semdinli. I said, 'I have no gold, and furthermore it is not my responsibility to pay for your smuggler.' They said, 'Yes, we know you have gold. Your husband, Taha, told us you have it.' Then Samira and Khan's wife told them that I had no gold, and that it was not their business. I was surprised that they asked me for gold, but I was very careful with these strangers. They left for Jalal Beck's house.

Cameron escaped from Sebete and made it to Semdinli the next day, leaving his two brothers, Yousif and Saman. Ahmad and Qasim had not told me that our three sons were still in Sebete village, and Cameron turned out to be a big support for me.

Malika description of her suffering in Semdinli—in her words:
I got your letter one day after coming to the house of Abdullah Khan in Semdinly, and you said in

the letter that I should go and ask for help from Jalal Beck, the famous Kurdish merchant.

Rezgar and I left the house of Abdullah Khan, and Abdullah Khan's wife guided us to the house of Jalal Beck. We walked to the nearby market, near the house of Abdullah Khan, and asked one of the shop owners for directions, and we walked up a steep hill. We became tired and sat down on the side of the road and began to cry. I was a refugee and afraid of Turkish security forces

Fortunately, my crying attracted the attention of a young Kurd, who stopped and asked if he could help; he knew we were Kurds and strangers. I told the young man, "We want to go to the house of Jalal Back." He told us to wait where we were, and Jalal would come by on the way to his merchandise office. After a short wait, a white car came toward us, and the young Kurd stood in the middle of the street and stopped Jalal's car.

The car window rolled down, and a young man got out and welcomed us. I spoke with him in Sorani Kurdish, but he wanted me to speak to him in Turkish. He wanted to learn about my problem. I told him, "We are asking your help to accept us as refugees—me, my husband, and my four children. We have fled from Saddam Hussein's regime, and we are here secretly."

Jalal told us, "Go to my mother in our house. I will come back. I will speak to the mayor and l ask him to let you stay here as refugees." I thanked him and thanked the young Kurd for their assistance. Jalal asked a man of his family to follow me to his house. We arrived at Jalal's house and met his mother who was a fine person. She made me sit close to her and looked me over carefully but respectfully, and she said, "God, you are from an ancient and respectable family that does not grieve and cry, and we will provide assistance to you and your family.

Jalal's mother asked one of the men in the family to slaughter a goat, and the man said they had already done so! Then she told him, "Kill the second goat for my respectful visitor Malika and her son Rezgar."

We waited few hours until the Mayor and a number of men of the Turkish state and Jalal Beck came into the visitors' huge room. Jalal's men served the Mayor and other men a fantastic and delicious lunch. The same kind of food was served for women too, in a women's hall.

I thanked God and ate, because I was hoping to get formal asylum. Rezgar was ashamed to start eating, but Jalal's mother said to Rezgar "Start eating, and I am like your grandmother." Rezgar began to eat fruits and to drink water and juice.

The Mayor and his men left the house. Jalal came and told us, "Turkish law forbids official acceptance of refugees, but you can stay in Semdinli secretly until the asylum law is changed."

With this news, I lost hope that we would gain asylum in Turkey. My son, Rezgar, and I thanked Jalal Beck and his mother, and we returned to the house of Abdullah Khan. There I noticed money had been stolen from my purse, and some of my clothes had also been stolen. I knew at once that the refugee who accompanied me to Abdulla Khan's house taken some of my money and my clothes. But I remained silent; I did not mention it.

Taha's judgement about gangs in Sebete was correct
I had told Cameron, in Sebete village, that Ahmad's family was a gang—and a danger to us. I was proved right; when I learned they had left Sebete and had come to Semdinli without telling my sons. They had promised to take care of the boys, and then when they arrived at Mullah Khan's house, they asked Malika for gold—like the criminals they were. God saved us from Ahmad's gang activities, and thereafter we ignored the Ahmad family and never again joined them.

My two sons, Yousif and Saman, were still in Sebete. I asked the Turkish police several times to arrest them in Sebete village so that they could join me in the jail. But the police did nothing. Nonetheless, my sons finally showed up at the jail. Mullah Khan had helped out, and had arranged a visit. Police opened a folder and began bombarding my sons with questions.

I asked Yousif how he had managed to escape and get to Semdinli. He said that Turkish soldiers had come looking for them, and one night two soldiers took

Yousif and Saman to an army base, about a thirty-minute walk from Madani's house. Upon arriving, the commander put them both in a room and began asking questions, trying to determine my whereabouts. The commander threatened to send them back to Iraq and hand them over to Iraqi soldiers. He was just playing games with their minds, but nonetheless my sons became very frightened. The next day they found a taxi and ultimately ended up in Semdinli, where they joined us in the jail.

On December 3, the police handed us over to Turkish soldiers, who said they were turning us over to Saddam's soldiers, on the Iraq border. They took us to a military station outside Semdinli in order, and said they would deliver us to Saddam's security people. On the first night there, Malika fainted. The officer called the nearest military unit and asked another officer to send a military doctor, which he did. The doctor arrived forty minutes later, and he turned out to be a great man. He kept us in the military station, ignoring the police order to hand us over to Saddam's people. Malika kept repeatedly fainting, and the military nurse kept injecting her with valium.

On December 7, soldiers transferred us to large Turkish military headquarters in Semdinli. They used Kurdish civilian trucks, not military trucks. They did not want our Kurd brothers to know what they were doing with us. While we were on the road to Semdinli military headquarter, the Kurdish truck driver asked me, "Why are you running away from Iraq to Turkey? Saddam is much better than the Turks" He felt sorry for us. He knew we were going to die at the Turkish-Iraq border.

The security officers dropped us off at the big Turkish military post in Semdinli. The next day, after lunch, I gave two Turkish soldiers ten dollars to contact a United Nations office by phone, to let officials know that we were refugees, headed to America.

On the morning of December 15, 1990, Turkish special soldiers prepared to put us on open military trucks, like cows. Malika was so sick—she thought she was going to die. I was resisting. Even though I was up against about fifty soldiers, I refused to obey their orders to get on the trucks. Soldiers pulled at my dusty and dirty teacher's suit, and one of them grabbed my jacket and tried to throw me onto the back of the truck. I continued to resist, and one soldier tore my jacket sleeve apart.

Soldiers pushed my sons, Malika, and me toward the trucks, and Malika fainted and fell to the ground. We had lost all hope, and then suddenly a good Turkish military general arrived and stopped the soldiers. He realized that my wife was in danger of dying. We all went back into the building, and the soldiers left.

The military doctor took us to his clinic room and gave Malika another injection, which revived her. But the tears flowed from her eyes. She said to me, "Are you OK?"

182

I said, "Yes, I am OK." But I was not OK. I could not come to grips with the reality that the Turkish government would want to hand over an entire family to the criminal Saddam. Malika asked about our sons, and about our situation. She thought the Turks had already handed us over to the Iraqis.

We tried to organize ourselves, pulling on shirts, jackets, and head hairs—and patting our clothes to get rid of the collected dust. We gathered our small escape bags, and then the army general came into the clinic room and handed us some papers. The papers informed us that we had been accepted as refugees, and that we would be reporting to the Hakkari Camp. It was unbelievably good news. The general had saved our lives. We thanked him profusely. We will never forget him. He made a humanistic decision and saved us from hanging, at the hands of the murderous Saddam.

Ch. 16- Turkish Refugee Prison Camps

Hakkari Refugee Camp

On December 15, 1990, the Turkish military general transferred us by civilian van to the refugee camp in Hakkari city. The camp was managed by Turkish intelligence and police forces. They put us in a room with two other families. The refugee camp consisted of an elementary school building, an old structure that lacked a heating system. Each room contained a coal stove, which when lit sent out bad fumes and toxins. The coal pollution caused many refugees to cough up blood. We asked for a doctor, but the response was harsh, disrespectful, and insulting.

We had tea, eggs, and bread for breakfast; rice and soup for lunch; and macaroni for supper. The camp had one toilet for men, and one toilet for women—each of which served about 100 refugees. There was a hall for cooking and eating, and refugees had to bring water into the camp for all their needs—cooking, drinking, and bathing. We obtained our water from a faucet outside the building. We were also responsible for supplying the officers with water, a difficult job. It was the cold winter season, and it snowed constantly. Some refugees lacked winter shoes, and their water carrying duties caused pain and suffering. My sons and I were among those who lacked winter shoes.

We were at the camp for about one month, from December 15, 1990, until January 14, 1991. We celebrated the New Year there, and some Christian refugees celebrated Christmas. My son, Yousif, celebrated his twentieth birthday at this deplorable camp. Officials regularly took us to the police station for interrogations. We were one of three or four Kurdish families, and we seemed to be subjected to more frequent questioning. The refugees were treated very badly, especially the Kurdish refugees. Turkey maintained the same hostility toward Kurds as did the Iraqis. The United Nations gave Turkey millions of dollars to treat refugees humanely, but the camp felt like a jail, and not a United Nations refugee camp.

What was our crime? I guess we were guilty of being refugees. The Turkish government held the view that all refugees were spies—except the Iraqi Turkmen, who received very favorable treatment. One of the officers, a man by the name of Hassan, had worked for the Hakkari police department. He told my son, Yousif, that Turkmen held special status, and a Turkmen could count on special treatment.

My son said, "Well, I am a Kurd and a Muslim. Does that have any meaning in your dictionary?"

The officer said, "Well, OK, you are a Muslim, but it is not like being both a Turkmen and a Muslim."

Then my son asked, "How do you feel about the Arab refugees?

The officer replied, "I hate them."

185

My son asked, "If you hate the Arab refugees, how do you feel about the Christian refugees?"

The officer said, "If I had the right, I would destroy them all."

Then my son said, "So you would destroy them the same way you destroyed the Kurds in Turkey. Is that what you mean?"

The officer asked, "What did you say?"

My son replied, "Nothing."

Security officer Ahmad Abi

There was in Hakkari camp an officer by the name of Ahmed Abi (Abi=elder brother), and he was very mean, especially to me. He would regularly come to our compound to see what we were up to—and to chat with an innocent young woman, who was with her husband. He would visit several times a day, and everyone knew that he had his eye on the young woman. Therefore, my family members would engage the woman in conversation whenever we saw the officer coming. We were trying save her from having to chat with this vile individual.

One day Ahmed Abi came in and started berating me for no reason. My son, Saman, saw what he was doing, and Saman seemed like he was about to attack the man. Ahmed noticed Saman's reaction, and he forced him into his office and delivered his insults there.

186

Turkmen families received very special treatment. They were given a monthly income, the best food, and also a supply of winter clothing. This treatment was delivered in a secretive fashion. The Turkish government did not want to provoke a revolt by the other non-Turkmen refugees. We were glad that our Turkmen brothers were getting help, but we also knew that some of them had been instructed to spy on the Kurdish refugees. The Turk's tried to develop hatred between Iraqi Kurds and Iraqi Turkmen. It was tactic they used as a political tool.

A coal stove heated our room, but we had to go outside the compound to obtain the coal. The coal smell was terrible, and we had to inhale the terrible fumes. We had no choice; the coal was our only source of warmth. The coal smoke blackened our ceiling and floor. The Turkmen refugees were provided oil stoves, and even electric stoves; they did not have to deal with the coal. We dealt with the coal, which sickened us.

After just a few days of exposure to the coal smoke, we all started coughing. My son, Yousif, fell ill and developed a bad cough. He also developed chest pains, fever, and a terrible headache—all due to the coal.

Our only point of contact was the foul Ahmed Abi. We told him that Yousif was sick and needed medical attention, but he simply declared that Yousif was not sick. Then Yousif started coughing up blood and developing terrible body aches. The pain was

187

unbearable, and it was heart wrenching to hear Yousif shouting and crying, as pain wracked his body.

There was a Kurdish doctor among the refugees, and at my request he came and examined Yousif and said that he needed immediate medical attention. Yousif was then taken to a hospital and treated. Ahmad Abi came with us on the first visit. As we entered the hospital, a Kurdish man, who was selling oranges out of a simple hand-push wagon, welcomed us in the Kurdish language. Ahmad Abi said, "Don't talk Kurdish to the refugees."

The Kurdish man said, "Can I not use my mother language?" Ahmed Abi put his hand over his handgun, but I immediately moved between the two, which allowed the Kurdish guy to escape. The police realized that taking us out of the camp, to the hospital, was a problem, so they began allowing the doctors to come into the camp once a week to treat sick refugees.

Tatvan refugee camp
On January 14, 1991, two big passenger buses arrived at the camp, and the refugees were told to pack up their belongings and wait outside, in the cold and snow. My family was the last to be called, and we didn't think we would make it onto the bus. I thought we might be returned to Iraq, but we were taken instead to the Tatvan city refugee camp. This was not a complete surprise. We had heard rumors that Saddam was starting another war, and people in Hakkari were afraid of a possible attack.

We stayed in the Tatvan refugee camp for two months, from January 14, 1991, March 15, 1991. We were treated well, but after about three weeks a problem developed. Seven of the two hundred refugees claimed that they were Turks, and they began getting special treatment. They were given winter coats and extra clothing, the best food, an income—and they were allowed to leave the camp. They were treated like Turkish citizens, not like Iraqi refugees.

The Kurdish refugees took note of all this and began to complain, asking why they were not given warm coats, bedding, decent food, and so on. The United Nations officials, who were monitoring the camp, had told the Turks that all food and supplies were to be distributed equally, but it wasn't happening. A group of policemen and the seven Turkmen refugees were getting the best and the most of the provisions. They were also meeting secretly in a room, where they would prepare lamb meat shish kabobs, accompanied by alcoholic beverages.

We did not seek to have the best or the most. Our goal was simply to get out of the camp, to find a new home, to continue our educations, and to become good members of American society.

Refugees had come in, and were coming in, from Iraq—mainly Kurds and Christians. My family members all spoke Turkish, as well as Kurdish, Arabic, and English; and so the Turkish government asked us to serve as translators. My sons Cameron, Saman, and Yousif began donating their time, helping refugees in any way they could. My son, Yousif, joined a team that was managing the kitchen, a food service that served approximately five hundred refugees each day. Many Kurdish refugee families continued to come in to the Tatvan camp.

Fake plan

One night we were awakened by sounds that made us think an earthquake had hit. We all sat on the edge of our beds, listening to the voices and shouts that permeated the camp. Strangers then came into our room, acting like barbarians and attackers. They ordered us into the hallway and made us stand there, as though we were hostages or prisoners of war. Then they began beating everyone in sight. I was lucky; I avoided their punches and kicks.

We learned later that these thugs were policemen and guards who had come looking for three Kurdish refugees who had supposedly escaped. But they knew where these three refugees were—they had helped them plan and execute their so-called "escape." The three refugees reappeared a few days later. They said they had been captured in a nearby village. But it was all a tactic, a way for the Turks to try and get information from the other Kurdish refugees. They wanted to know who was actually planning an escape. They assumed that anyone trying to escape was a Saddam spy.

United Nations and journalists

A few days later, United Nations officials visited the camp, accompanied by several journalists who were reporting on camp conditions. The Turkish police and security people went on their best behavior, trying to convey that they were treating refugees in a caring and humane fashion. They managed to communicate an image that did not match the reality we were seeing every day. It was a false image. They could fool the UN officials and reporters, but I know that they did not fool God.

My son, Yousif, who worked in the kitchen, said that the workers were ordered to prepare the best food possible, and to provide large and varied servings. This was a departure from the regular servings of rice and soup. With reporters present, refugees were served rice and soup—but each was also given half a chicken, together with a salad and fruit (apples and oranges). Following the dinner serving, each was given a piece of pie, with hot tea or coffee. This was a great day for the refugees—it was like a feast. The refugees prayed that the reporters would come every day.

The reporters interviewed refugees, who generally made positive comments about their treatment. No one wanted to create trouble. Many, however, asked how long they would remain in the camp. The reporters came to our compound, accompanied by Turkish police and security officials. We spoke to Turkish, English, US, and European reporters about the Turkish government's treatment of us, and of the other refugees. The UN people asked questions. How did we get to Turkey? Who helped us escape? Would we return if Saddam Hussein were deposed?

As the reporters prepared to leave, and the police and security people had left, one journalist, a man from the Netherlands, continued to conduct interviews. My son, Yousif, then got into a conversation (in English) about the great players Holland had produced and how the Netherlands had won the European Cup in 1988, beating the Russians. Yousif knew the names of the great players from the Netherlands—Marco Van Bastin and Rod Goleot—and the journalist enjoyed the conversation.

Separation of husbands and wives in Tatvan camp, 1991
We sometimes talked about Saddam. Some of the police and security officials seemed to know that I was not pro-Turkish, and that I might be a threat of some kind. Some Tatvan refugees had earlier launched a protest against the Turkish management operations, which were at times inhumane. This did not help our situation; it did not improve the treatment.

Refugees continued to stream into the Tatvan camp, a consequence of Saddam's war in Kuwait. The Turkish government separated Saddam's former army men from their wives and children, and shipped them to an army base in Siirt city, about a two-hour drive from Tatvan. The wives and children were forced to stay in the Tatvan camp, alone, without their husbands and fathers. Many husbands refused to leave their families, and this brought on beatings by armed Turkish soldiers.

I clearly remember one husband who refused to be separated from his wife and two-year-old daughter. He was badly beaten in front of his wife and daughter, and his face was bloodied. I saw him lying outside in the snow. He was later carried off in a truck to Siirt.

The refugees at the Siirt military base were further beaten and tortured, and many wound up with serious injuries. Turkish soldiers tortured male Iraqi refugees with electric shocks, and they would beat them with bone-breaking force. One a refugee Kurd, by the name of Iskander, was given electric shocks until he finally lost his mind. Soldiers repeatedly tortured a man named Firyad, finally breaking his arm.

The women and children left behind would cry and plead with authorities to return their husbands and fathers, but to no avail. This treatment by the Turks of innocent individuals reminded me of the way Hitler had persecuted the Jews before and during World War II.

I was the oldest man left in the Tatvan camp, so families would ask me to communicate their needs to camp officials. They would also ask me to help resolve problems they were having with one another. I had the opportunity to speak briefly to an international journalist. I asked him to take a message to the United Nations officials—ask them to move refugees to various countries, so that young people could continue their educations, and not rot in refugee camps.

Daily routine

The entertainment mainly consisted of television watching, from eleven o'clock in the morning to approximately eight o'clock in the evening. After nine o'clock, everyone had to be in their beds. Showers were available in the rooms, but the water was cold. Table tennis was available, and my son, Yousif, organized two tournaments that involved 500 refugees. It seemed to relieve stress and delay thoughts about what might come next. For my son, it was a great way to express himself without fear of retaliation. He took first place in one tournament and second place in another. Another refugee organized a chess tournament in which Yousif took a second.

One of the Turkish security officers was a great table tennis player. He had watched my son play and was very impressed with his game. My son would compete with him, and this led to some kind of a relationship, even though my son beat him most of the time.

One Turkmen refugee, one of those who received special treatment, got into an argument with my son, who might have been well advised to just walk away. People like that, we learned, were evil, and had many connections. But my son was not about to walk away and shortly after the fight broke out he noticed a cut on the fourth finger of his left hand. His fingernail had been separated from the flesh. Following the altercation, he

194

went to the nurse, who gave him shots and pulled off the fingernail. He received treatment for the next two weeks.

Ch. 17- Escorted from Prison Camp

Tatvan camp

Camp Tatvan resembled a jail. Refugees were prohibited from contacting United Nations representatives in their quest to begin anew life in another country, in any country but Iraq. We were visited one day by a group of Turkmen, political and security people who were trying to identify Kurds and provide a report to the Turkish government. Several days later the camp director said to me, "Prepare your family." I asked him why. He said, "Your family is going to Diyarbakir refugee camp. This camp is crowded; it has too many refugees."

I was surprised, but I had no choice, so I began preparing my family for the move. We had no money. I was forced to sell my beautiful camera to a Kurdish worker in the camp for a low price. I observed that other Turkmen families were feeling sorry for us. They had had meetings with the Turkish police and security people, and they knew what was in store for us. All the other refugees respected us, even the camp director.

On March 15, 1991, we loaded ourselves into a van, which was waiting for us at the main gate. Two policemen armed with machine guns also came on board, and two minibuses filled with armed police joined us, one in front of the van and one in back. Refugees in the camp waved at us, and refugees in the van waved back at others still in the camp, until they were out of

196

sight. Then we fell silent. We were going someplace, but it wasn't to Diyarbakir. We had again been lied to.

Siirt security jail

Our convoy neared a city, and we could see it was Siirt. We reached the city, and after a fifteen-minute drive through winding streets, the convoy stopped at a dark security building. The policemen in our van got out, and our driver, a Turkish Kurd, asked me, "Why did you talk to journalists?" He seemed sad, and I wanted to learn more, but the police were nearby, and I couldn't continue the conversation.

The police ordered us around as though we were hostages. "Come out from the van now," one said. We had no idea where we were headed. The security people at the building yelled at us, ordering us to enter the building. Malika was walking quickly, and she tripped and fell, and injured her elbow. I ran to her side, but I could not help her. Then she stood up like a lion, and bravely walked into the building. We were so tired, and we'd had nothing to eat or drink, from the previous noon until the van trip ended at sunset.

We spent one night in that building, and we learned to our sorrow that we were going to be turned over to Saddam's soldiers. The jail provided no beds and no food, but we didn't care. We assumed that we were about to die on the Iraqi border. I lay down on my back on the cold cement floor of that dark jail cell, and put my head on a small bag. I recalled the words of the first president Bush. "Iraqi people," he had said, "don't listen to your leader, Saddam, because he wants to fight the world."

These words had motivated me to get my family to Turkey. I knew that Turkey and the United States were allies, and I thought the Turks would respect me, since I was wishing to get to America, and since I detested Saddam and his brutal regime. I tried to sleep, but with no bed, pillow, or blanket, sleep would not come. I covered Malika with my two shirts, to keep her warm, and then she took the shirts and covered my youngest son, age eleven. It was a harsh, sleepless night, and in the morning we saw that the building was surrounded by the same policemen who had accompanied us on the van, on the trip from Tatvan to Siirt.

Silopi police jail

Police ordered us into a van, after a morning breakfast of a few black olives, some cheese, and some bread crusts—no tea or coffee, just leftover food. We got into the van, and into the middle of a convoy consisting of Turkish military trucks and small military tanks. The vehicles were filled with solders carrying machine guns, and with military dogs. We all had dry mouths and pale faces, and we remained silent, wondering where we were headed. We had lost hope. We saw a sign pointing toward Iraq, and my poor wife, Malika, fainted. We knew we were on our way to Iraq and certain death.

The police would tell us nothing. I asked them to take us to a hospital, so Malika could get some medical

198

attention. The police called their office, and then all the vehicles stopped, and my sons were placed in a civilian police van. Malika, two policemen, a driver, and I went on to Cizre city in a van. We found a small clinic, and a nurse gave Malika an injection to wake her up. We then left the clinic and continued our sad journey to the city of Silopi. We met our sons at the security officers' room. We knew that Silopi was on the Iraqi border. Malika had returned to a normal state, and she began reading our Holy book. She knew were just a few miles from the Iraq border.

The security civilian officer asked me, "Are you Kurdish or Turkmen?"

I replied, "We are Kurdish, but what difference does it make?"

My wife and sons looked at me, and he said, "The difference is that I would not exchange one fingernail of a Turkmen for the lives of thousands of Kurds."

Then I became silent, but I thought to myself, "You have no religion and no humanity."

I also thought to myself, how could these people have such hatred toward the Kurds? We are a population of at least 40,000,000. Do we not have a right to our own country? Do humans simply follow the law of the jungle, where the strong eat the weak?

Evening came, and we decided to fast in observance of Ramadan, which would begin the next day. The security officer put us in a jail, to await the knife that we were sure the butcher Saddam would wield.

Habor River at night, March 17, 1991

On March 17, 1991, at 1:00 a.m., on the first day of Ramadan, trucks, soldiers, and dogs surrounded our jail in the Kurdish city of Silopi. Turkish police made walkie-talkie connection with Iraqi army forces, and told them to get ready; the family was on its way. Malika raised the Quran to the sky and asked God for help. The wicked policeman tried to slap her, but he missed and hit the Quran. At this moment, Malika again became very emotional and fainted, and I shouted loudly for a doctor.

Police came, and my sons and I carried Malika to the civilian police van, which then took her to a one-room clinic, where a nurse gave her an injection and revived her. We returned to Silopi, and at this point we had lost all control of our lives. Our destiny was in the hands of the great Lord. Malika was the only one who was crying, but she was not crying for herself; she was crying for me and our sons. The nearby Silopi residents heard our voices and noticed the dirty military trucks— and the smoke, voices, and dust—and they felt sympathy for our plight. The coming morning would bring the first day of Ramadan. Night came, and we were placed on an open military truck. The wind and cold, and our empty stomachs, were killing us, but who cared—we were on our way to certain death.

We arrived at a Kurdish river called Khabor, which formed part of the Turkish-Iraqi border. The Turkish commanding officer ordered me into the river and told me to find a shallow spot. I was the only family member who could swim. I waded into the water in my dusty and dirty teacher's suit, and I felt the cold water biting at me, but I was determined to stay strong and not show weakness.

I tried to find a shallow place, but couldn't locate one. The officer told me to get out of the river and onto the bank, on the Turkish side. I came out, and all sons and my wife slapped at me, trying to get rid of the water on my suit. Their eyes were filled with tears. I said to them, "Don't worry. I am OK."

We were supposed to go to another location on the Kurdish river Khabor, but the officer's truck would not start. He couldn't get it started. He then got a call from Ankara, and he was able, by the name of God, to start it. By the grace of God, Malika's prayers may have been answered. They put us back onto the open truck, continuing to treat us like animals, and we headed toward Silopi. I asked one friendly soldier, "Why we are going back to Silopi, and not to our final destination with the Iraqi army, to be killed?" The soldier just shook his head back and forth, indicating that he had no idea why the plan had been changed.

Do you believe in miracles? At the same time that the truck had broken down and was disabled for an

201

hour, the Iraqi army unit, the one that was supposed to receive us, had been crushed by a Kurdish military force, part of the Peshmerga. It was an uprising in Iraqi Kurdistan against Saddam!

Silopi again and Ata Hotel

We arrived back at the police station in Silopi at 4:00 a.m., and were transported to the Ata Hotel, in the suburbs of Silopi. We went into the hotel, but it was vacant, nobody there but us. There were just a few rooms in that very small hotel. We slept soundly the entire night. We were still fasting. I left the hotel room, to see what was going on. I walked down a flight of stairs, but then saw police in the lobby, and so I went back to our room.

I returned to the lobby, and asked if I could call my childhood friend, Ghazi, in Istanbul. The police gave me permission to make the call, and the owner provided a phone. I wanted Ghazi to contact Turkish political figures and get them to stop the murderous plan to send us back to Iraq. I reached Ghazi's house, and his son answered, and he was loudly weeping. I said, "Who are you, and why are you crying?

He said, "I am Ghazi's son, and I am crying because my dad died and his body is still in the house"

I began crying and yelling, and then a man took the phone and said, "Who are you?"

I said, "I am Taha, a childhood friend of Ghazi's."

The man said, "What do you need?"

I said, "Who are you?"

He replied, "I am Hasan Salih, Ghazi's brother."

I was still crying. I said, "Do you know who I am?" He said he did, and I said, "Please we need help. The Turkish Government is trying to hand me and my family over to Saddam. We are helpless. We can't do anything."

I don't know exactly why I decided to call Ghazi's home, but I think God ordered me to call, and to see if I could find help in Istanbul. I thanked the policeman and hotel owner for helping me make the call, and I returned to our room and shared the sad news about Ghazi. But we knew that the smuggler Hussein Salih and his brother, Ghazi, had given me bad information when they told me to use Turkey as a path to America. They wanted us to suffer.

The small hotel sat in a suburb of Silopi, on the main road to Istanbul. That evening the Kurdish hotel owner of the hotel prepared a delicious meal for us, but we were still fasting, except for my youngest son. The police started giving us food the next day.

On March 25, the police transferred us to Hajji Hussein Hotel in downtown Silopi. We were allowed to watch television in the lobby, and on March 31 we watched a report about the millions of Kurds who had been displaced, and had moved from Iraq to Turkey and Iran. We saw how the Kurdish people in Turkey had aided the Iraqi Kurds. The American secretary of state had visited some Kurdish immigrants on a rainy field in Turkey. He told them that he would provide immediate aid, and helicopters later dropped off thousands of tents and of food boxes, helping people protect themselves from the cold, and relieving their hunger. Americans also provided health care aid, and halted the killing of refugees who were escaping from Iraq and going to Turkey.

Our hearts went out to the Kurdish immigrants, but nearly a thousand Iraqi Christian immigrants also arrived in Silopi. United Nations workers made a camp for them and gave them tents. After one week at the Haji Hussien Hotel, Turkish police transferred us to an open camp. We completed Ramadan there.

On April 16, 1991, the first day of Eid Al-Fitir, I asked police to take me to the feast day Morning Prayer service. I came back from mosque under police escort to our tent. We prepared Eid A-Fitir food, and we prayed for our family and for all good people in the world. With our eyes raining tears, we asked God to help us, and we prayed that our dream to find freedom in America would be realized.

On April 22, 1991, at 10:00 a.m., Turkish police and intelligence officials readied some big modern busses at the camp, and told us to pack our bags and prepare for a trip. We were happy. We were going to Istanbul to the United Nations offices, where refugees were given permission to enter European countries, America, and Canada. I said to my wife, "It looks like God heard my prayer this morning, and he is now going to send us to America."

Turkish intelligence people approached us with papers listing the names of those who would take the bus to Istanbul. We were excited, but then we found that we were not on the list of those who were to board the bus. Instead we were told to board an old ugly van. My son said, "Do you think this old nasty van will get us to Istanbul?" I took a deep breath and said to God, "Please you know better than Taha. I want to go to Istanbul and then to America, but maybe it is not a good plan for us at this time."

Police and security people entered our van, and the busses began moving out of the camp. Our poor ugly van followed. The busses turned left and headed toward Istanbul. Our van turned right and headed toward Silopi. We reached Silopi, and were dropped off at a hotel that belonged to Ata's brother.

We were overcome with sadness. I was very worried about Malika's health. The Kurds at the hotel also seemed sad. They seemed to know that something bad was going to happen to us, but nobody was able to converse with us. Turkish police were present, carrying machine busses, and they had the power. The family of the hotel owner sent us Kurdish food. I approached the owner to thank him, but I saw that he was arguing with the Turkish police about Kurdish rights in Turkey.

I met a German medical doctor in the hotel lobby, and I asked him if he would examine Malika. He checked her blood pressure and heart rate, and said that she needed immediate attention and should be taken to the emergency room. I told him that we were basically in a jail and could not leave the hotel. So Malika continued to lie in her bed, sleepless and suffering. We did not know why we were being held in the hotel, but we felt that our dream of reaching America was coming to an end, and we were sad.

As we struggled with our pain, we heard a knock on the door. It was the police, who said, "Hurry everyone, wake up, get your bags out and prepare to leave." I stood up and put on my teacher's suit jacket. I put the left lens of my broken glasses to my eye, and turned to see what time it was. It was 2:00 a.m., April 23, 1991.

Malika prepared herself and told our sons to be brave, and then several policemen escorted us from the hotel. We wanted to thank the hotel owner, but were unable to do so. We were hostages. We were then directed to get onto an open civilian truck filled with cow manure.

Sirnak, the Kurdish city in Turkey

We were forced to sit on piles of cow manure that felt like cushions. We sat with our backs against one another, trying to stay warm. The cold wind was hitting us, and we didn't know where we were going. Police were in the truck, and a police car was leading the way, as we sped along the narrow highway. The cold wind and the truck's exhaust fumes were killing us and making it impossible to hear and converse. From time to time I would ask Malika and sons how they were doing, and they would say, "We are OK, don't worry."

Dawn came, and the sun warmed us, and we found ourselves in a city called Sirnak. The truck passed through a wide gate and stopped at the back of a security building. We jumped from the truck and headed toward the bathroom to relieve ourselves and wash our faces. I heard a policeman say, "If I were the decision maker, I would immediately shoot that Kurdish family like Hitler killed the Jews."

We didn't know each other, and I wondered why he would say such a thing. We thought that we would be provided food and water, and instead they insulted us. We were angry, but we did not worry because we were on a "Long Road to Freedom."

The truck left Sirnak and was joined by military tanks. We neared an area that contained two million Kurds, refugees who had fled Iraq after the first Gulf War, escaping Saddam and his chemical weapons. We were hoping to be dropped off there, but instead we

207

headed toward a huge mountain that was part of the Iraqi border, or more specifically Iraqi Kurdistan's border. The truck stopped, and we exited. Soldiers and one Turkish officer also left their trucks, each carrying a machine gun. We thought they were going to shoot us, and we were ready for it; we did not show any fear. The officer said, "Now go to Iraq and don't come back to Turkey." My wife Malika responded and said, "God's misfortune on all of you. We will go to Kurdistan." The officer was a good guy, and he gave us the right to be sad.

So, that's the story of what happened to us in Turkey. While there we felt no hatred toward Turkey, but from thereon I felt that I had the full right to describe what we had experienced in that country. The cruel treatment of my family has become deeply embedded in my memory, and I can't forget the ways in which Turks brought suffering to my family.

After we had been released and were together in in free Kurdistan, I said to my family, "We are winners now, even though we have lost much." We lost the $45,000 that we paid the smugglers. We lost our house and my job, and my retirement benefits. My sons lost many years in which they could have been pursuing their educations. We lost time and were forced to deal with six months of threats and insults and detention. And we seemed to have lost a bright future.

But I knew we had to continue our journey over these mountains. We had to hold on to our dream. We had to trust God, and not be ruled by Turks and other oppressive forces. I prayed that God would help Turkey develop ways to treat Kurds and other refugees more humanely. We reached Kurdistan, and we hugged one another, tears in our eyes. And we decided that we would not give up on our quest for freedom. We would fight to reach the USA—and freedom.

Ch. 18- US Army Refugee Camp

Burned bus and French soldiers

On the morning of April 23, 1991, we began climbing our mountain, and as we walked, my sick wife seemed to gain strength. She walked along briskly, like a deer, my hero sons close behind. We finally made it to the top, a nine-hour trek, but with no food to sustain us. It was nighttime when we reached the peak, but we could see the flat green land below, a sight that cheered us and gave us strength

We discovered some food lying on the ground, fare that I'm sure had been dropped by U.S. military airplanes in America's effort to help the Kurdish refugees. My son Saman found a juice can, and we were glad to have found something to quench our thirst, but the juice had a bitter taste, and we threw it away, not realizing it was grapefruit juice.

We continued our journey and rain began to fall; but God was great, and we came to a spot that contained about fifty bombed and burned out cars—and a huge wrecked bus. We yelled and shouted, trying to determine if anyone was present, but there was no response, and so we decided to move into the bus. It was a total wreck, but to us it looked like a king's house, a shelter and a fortress that could protect us from the cold rain and dangerous animals.

We spent the entire night in that bus, and in the morning I walked over to a nearby stream to wash my face and to pray. Suddenly I heard the sound of a vehicle; it seemed to be approaching us. We made a line on the paved road, and quickly spotted six or seven military vehicles moving toward us. They slowed down and stopped some distance away, thinking perhaps that we were enemies. Then they saw that we were civilians and needed help, and we recognized that they were French soldiers.

French soldiers

The soldiers put down their machine guns and approached us. We put up our hands, and asked who they were and where they were going. They were French soldiers, part of a French Army unit that was assisting a Kurdish aid program called Operation Provide Comfort. They were headed to the city of Zakho, and we asked if they would take us to an American camp in the Kurdish city of Zakho. They agreed, and gave us sodas and food. We boarded the truck, a clean vehicle with fixed seats, and after a four-hour drive we reached the outskirts of the American camp.

I indicated that we wanted to stop there, and we exited the truck, thanking the soldiers for their help. We thanked God too for helping us to find the US camp. The French vehicle would have taken us to the center of Zakho, but it was filled with Saddam's military and security people, and our lives would again have been in great danger. God was with us. We saw the US Army camp, just before reaching Zakho's downtown area.

We cut through a wheat field and reached the main camp gate, where a few American soldiers were on guard. We asked for help, and the soldiers understood that we had faced serious problems, and still were. An officer, Lt. Baker, appeared, and we told him we were homeless, and that we had been in Turkey from November 10, 1991, until just the previous night, April 24, 1991.

The officer left, but then quickly returned with a map that he spread out on the ground. He also dropped to the ground, as did we, and we pointed out the Tatvan camp where we had spent many days. I also pointed out my city, Kirkuk. The officer stood up, and again left us, but soon returned with this news: "Turkey did not accept you, but we accept you." He ordered his soldiers to give us sodas and food, and they set up a nice new tent for us, one that could have accommodated three families. The tent was just outside the camp, and empty because it was still under construction.

U.S. Army tent
We slept soundly that night, and then sometime before dawn, I heard a voice calling, "Taha, Taha." It was the voice of the officer who had provided our tent. "Are you alright?" he asked. I said that were fine. He said, "We are protecting you, because we know that some of Saddam's soldiers are in downtown Zakho."

I said, "Thank you, Sir," and he left. I knew that Zakho's downtown was only a mile away, and I was

212

grateful for this protection. I went back to sleep, knowing I needed to restore some of my energy.

The next day, my sons helped the soldiers set up more tents inside the camp, to accommodate other refugees who would soon be arriving. The soldiers gave us a generous supply of food, but we had no pots or dishes. One old man from Zakho approached me and greeted me, and I gave him a bottle of oil, two plastic bags of rice, and one small box of raisins. He then went home and brought back pots, dishes, spoons, and other utensils. We prepared a nice meal over a fire of wild bushes, accompanied by boxes of clean water.

Zakho and hope
Within two weeks, helicopters had brought 15.000 refugees to the camp. We moved inside, and I provided assistance to the refugees, working closely with the Americans. I also wrote letters to American officials, asking for asylum in America, for me and my family members.

By June of 1991, the refugees were able to return to their homes, but we were not able to return to Kirkuk, for several reasons:

Kirkuk was under the control of Saddam. It was not in a no fly zone, as was Erbil and other Kurdish cities.

I had given an interview that had been broadcast on Turkish television. I had severely criticized Saddam, and

213

I was a target for his security people, who had recorded the interview.

I had sold my house in Kirkuk to pay the smuggler, and at this point I had no money.

So, I rented a room in a Kurdish house in Zakho, and I began working with the Kurdish Democratic Party, helping protect citizens and merchants. I became director of the night guards, many of which I hired. We were able to protect people's shops and houses, and I carefully supervised my guards, correcting our mistakes as we went along and further developing our services. My PDK leaders were Mustansir and Muetasim, and both were from Zakho.

My sons and I were able to meet members of a French organization called Medecins Du Monde, a medical unit that was assisting refugees. Then a medical journalist with that unit, a woman by the name of Michelle Lavoisier, spoke to Colonel James Jones and described our situation. The Colonel invited me to see him, and on July 13 I visited him in his office. I told him I had been a mathematics teacher in Iraq, and I described the pain and suffering we had experienced, and how our lives had been repeatedly endangered—simply because we were Kurds. The Colonel then delivered good news. He said he would send a refugee application for us to America, but he said, "The answer may not come for two or more months."

On July 14, at 8:00 a.m., my wife, Malika, and my son, Rezgar, and Malika's brother left Zakho to visit Malika's mother, Talatt, in Kirkuk. Malika had not seen her mother since November 11, 1990, when we fled Iraq. We knew there was time for the visit, since the Colonel had told me that it would take one or two months to get a response to our application for asylum.

At 10:00 a.m. on the same day, the Colonel asked to see me immediately, and I met with him in his office, where he gave me great news. "Congratulations. America accepted you and tomorrow at noon you will fly in my helicopter to Turkey and after completing some paperwork, you will go to America."

I realized at that moment I had a mistake by letting Malika and Rezgar go to Kirkuk. I told the Colonel what I had done and asked for his help. I said, "Please would you hold up the flight time until 6:00 p.m. tomorrow? I thought Malika would have time to visit her mother. As you know, Kirkuk is still under Saddam's control, and it is dangerous for me to go there; it's possible that I could get captured. Please, if I don't arrive by 6:00 p.m., then would you just help my other three sons who are in Zakho? I will try my best to be with my wife and four sons in Zakho at 6:00 p.m., in order to fly to Turkey." The general's eyes filled with tears, and so did mine

He said, "OK, the flight will wait for you until 6:30 p.m."

215

I went back to my tent, and I told my three sons, "Please, you are heroes. Be strong. Respect all people. Reach your goals by education. If I do not come back from Kirkuk by 6:00 p.m., then you three have to go to America. The general will take care of you."

They said, "No, we will stay in Zakho and wait for mother and Rezgar and you."

Dangerous trip to Kirkuk
On July 15 at 3:00 a.m., I left my three sons and went to the transportation area in Zakho. I spotted a car with a sleeping driver inside, and I quietly rapped on the window. The driver opened one eye, saw me, and then opened the other eye. He sat up and looked at me, then at his watch. He may initially have thought I was a robber, but I was wearing my teacher's suit, and I didn't look like a criminal. He rolled down the window and said, "What is going on?"

I said, "Please, take me to Mosul city."

He said to me, "I have not enough passengers, and the time is so early."

I said, "You don't need passengers, because I will pay the complete cost for transportation from Zakho to Mosul."

He said, "The time is so early, and I can't do it."

216

I replied, "It is an emergency, and I will pay you double the cost." He accepted that offer and opened the front passenger door, and we departed. We drove for forty minutes and then stopped at the Ba'ath checkpoint in Faidah, a city that was still under Saddam's control. The Arab security man approached our car, and I said, "Hello," using an Arabic slang expression. He looked at me with a surprised expression, and waved us through. Thanks to God, I passed Saddam's dangerous security man.

As we moved down the road, I began conversing with the driver, informing him that I was serving as the director of night guards in Zakho city. I wanted the driver to feel comfortable and safe with me. We arrived at Mosul, but then I said, "Please continue driving, to Kirkuk."

He replied, "It is impossible, because Kirkuk is very far for me. I will not have passengers going back from Kirkuk to Mosul, and I have to buy three big pots of yogurt in Mosul for our yogurt shop owner, Hajji Isamel, in Zakho. He needs it this morning, in order to sell it."

I told him, "I have a solution." I am going to Kirkuk to bring back my wife and son, Rezgar, to Zakho before 1:00 p.m., which is a deadline for me to catch our flight to America."

The driver, surprise on his face, said, "To America?"

I told him, "Yes, to America." I was trusting that he would not hand me over to Saddam's soldiers for money, and said to him, "I will pay you double the cost and a tip for this round trip between Zakho and Kirkuk."

He said to me, "If you will help me buy the yogurt, I will pay another Zakho driver to deliver it." He ended with the remark, "You have solved all the problems that I have."

We took care of the yogurt issue, and went on to the city of Erbil. I wanted to stop in Erbil, to visit my sister's house and to see if Malika was there. But instead I decided to go on to Kirkuk. The checkpoints were weak, and God saved me from the Ba'ath party. We arrived in Kirkuk, and I found Malika's mother's house. I knocked on the door, and hiding my face from the neighbors, I waited. Malika then opened the door, surprised and confused, but God saved her from a heart attack. Rezgar, my son, was there, too.

We had morning tea and breakfast, and we prepared to leave Kirkuk forever. My mother-in-law, Talatt, came close to me, and she was so sad. She said to me, "Take care of Malika."

I said to her, "I will put Malika on my head, and she is my Queen." I bent and kissed Talatt's hand, knowing that this would be our final meeting.

From Kirkuk to Zakho

On July 15, 1991, were finally together, headed toward Zakho, but my wife said "Let's go see your mother first in Kirkuk."

I said, "My heart is burning for her, but what can I do? My sons are in Zakho. The general and his helicopter are waiting for us, and I am sure many of Saddam's security officers are around my mother's house."

I knew we had to return quickly, and so we drove safely out of Kirkuk. We arrived in Erbil, a safe place for me, and then arrived in Zakho for noon time prayers. My entire family was thrilled—finally we were again together and headed for a new world

Before we met with Colonel James Jones, Michelle Lavoisier and the Medecins Du Monde crew met with us, and awarded us a Medecins Du Monde attestation and pin, a token that expressed their gratitude and appreciation for our services to the organization, for our help in serving as interpreters for the U.S. Marines, and for helping with the resettlement of thousands of Kurdish refugees.

We reported to the Colonel's office, and he was happy to see us and to see that we had safely returned. Colonel Jones gave me our papers and told me that the US ambassador would come to my hotel, and that I must give him the brown envelope that contained the papers. I thanked Colonel James Jones profusely. I had developed the greatest respect for him, and words could not adequately express my gratitude. I said myself, "God is making these arrangements. I am following His orders, and now my family will be safe."

Ch. 19- Flying from Zakho to Silopi

To Silopi by U.S. military helicopter,

On July 15, 1991, at 4:00 p.m., my family and I flew by helicopter to Silopi, to a temporary American helicopter base. This was the first time we had flown, and as the helicopter lifted up and began moving, we were able to look down at Kurdistan. And tears filled our eyes, as we thought about our roots, and the pain we felt on separating from those familiar roots. It was like pulling up an old tree from the ground. An American soldier noticed our tears and the pain in our faces, and he said, "More patience, guys. You are headed toward freedom, and Kurdistan is yours."

We dried our eyes, and the helicopter soon began descending to the base in Silopi, a Kurdish city in Turkey that was settled by Turks following World War I. We landed and exited the helicopter, and this time Silopi welcomed us. But we recalled the vivid images we had retained from that March night in 1991, the Eve of Ramadan. We recalled the Turkish security officer, the Turkish police jail, the Turkish soldiers with their dogs and machine guns, the open military trucks that took us to Habor River on a cold night. I recalled how the Turk officer ordered me into Habor River, at midnight, on April 21, 1991. We all recalled how Turkish police awakened us at 2:00, took us from our hotel and put us on an open truck, as though we were animals—and then took us to an unknown destination on a freezingly cold night.

221

Those memories and more washed over us, and then the memories faded, as we realized we were in Silopi—no longer under Turkish authority, but safe under the protection of an American leader, Colonel James Jones.

American military airmen directed us to a spot on the base where we could rest and gather ourselves, and there we met five or six Kurdish families who were also headed to America. We met the family of Matti Khoshaba, a well known Kurdish English teacher, and he volunteered to help my family and others acquire some English language proficiency. He continued to do so throughout our journey.

After a short rest, American military folks prepared a wonderful dinner for us, and then set up tents with nice clean beds. We slept soundly, dreaming of America and the peace and freedom we had long sought. We awoke to the sight of golden sun rays, and our hearts were filled with happiness, as were the hearts of the other families. Out of four million Kurds, our family was one of seven that had (in 1991) gained refugee status

From Silopi to Ankara
On July 16, 1991, American military officials put us on a big bus, where we were greeted by a representative of the American embassy in Turkey. We set out for Ankara, and then stopped in Adana at a roadside restaurant. As I entered the restaurant, I heard a voice call out,"Mr. Taha." I looked to my right and saw a Turkish policeman from Silopi coming toward me. I

222

expected the worst, but he extended his hand and then hugged me and said, "I was so sorry for your family's sad situation on Ramadan eve in Silopi."

I replied, "Your Turkish country is Islamic, but now you see that a non-Islamic country is taking care of us, because we are refugees and are weaker than butterflies." He was a good guy, and he said he would pray for us, pray that we would successfully reach our goal—to get to America. The United Nations official who was accompanying us seemed pleased that this Turkish policeman offered his prayers. We then had some delicious shish kabobs, after which we boarded the bus and continued on toward Ankara, the capital.

After an all night drive we reached Ankara. The bus stopped at the United Nations building to pick up an official, who took us to the Konia Hotel. We checked in and showered, and went to a nearby restaurant for lunch. At 4:00 p.m. The Honorable American Ambassador visited us at our hotel. He was glad to see us, and we were honored by his visit. I gave him the folder that Colonel Jones had given me in Zakho camp.

We stayed at the Konia hotel for a week and then moved to the Turan Palas hotel, owned by a Kurd named Ibraheem. We were free to go out and visit parks, and markets. We encountered a family we had met at the Tatvan camp, and one member said, "When you left Tatvan camp, the director met with all the refugees and let us know that Turkey was going to turn over Muhammad's family to Saddam's soldiers at the Iraqi border that night. He warned us, and said that we let the best family die that night at the Iraq border." That same family told us that one of their daughters had held the Quran Al-Kareem and prayed for God to save us all. We thanked the daughter for her prayers.

We had a wonderful time in Ankara. Several times we went with other refugees to Turkish offices to request visas, but they refused to give us permission to remain in Turkey, and they also tried to end the American help we were receiving. But the US officials were on our side, and we completed the paperwork.

From Ankara to Istanbul to Brussels

On September 25, after a seventy-day wait in Ankara, we boarded a small Turkish plane and flew to Istanbul, and then by a huge plane flew on to Brussels, the capital of Belgium. At the Brussels airport, we left the plane to use a bathroom and rest area. I tried to wash my face, but I couldn't operate the faucet, and a restroom worker had to open it for me. My sons laughed at me. I guess I seemed like a wild man who couldn't use simple technology. I was embarrassed, but I knew my sons were just teasing me in a good natured way.

I blamed Saddam Hussein. He stole Kurdistan's oil income and spent it on chemical weapons and military arms for terrorists around the world. His regime did not bring technology into Iraq. Instead, his brutal regime brought sadness and mass destruction. He used chemical weapons on the Kurdish city of Halabja, killing 300,000 innocent Kurds.

224

After our airplane had been refueled and serviced, we again took off, this time for New York. The smokers on the plane made people uncomfortable, but we reached New York, and I was amazed at what I saw. I said to my family, "Look at this. Look at the developments in America and compare them to Iraq's." My youngest son Rezgar, who was age eleven, laughed at me and said, "Ask Saddam!"

I desperately needed to go to the bathroom, and I found a restroom. I started to enter, but then quickly retreated. It was a women's restroom. I was shocked and said to myself, "Oh God, the restroom is for women." I was so lucky that no one saw me trying to use the women's bathroom. It would have been a disaster, and it would have shamed all of us.

As we walked through the airport, I said to my family, "Do you remember when I told you that we are winners, even though Turkish thugs had escorted us to the Iraqi-Kurdistan border—and didn't allow us to wait and meet with United Nations people, so that we could gain refugee status. See, we are now in America. See how our dream has come true!" We then reported to the immigration office at the New York airport.

New York City, USA

On September 25, we met with an immigration officer at the airport, and we received our refugee cards. The officer then led us to a bus. We probably looked like uncivilized people, as we looked around in amazement at the buildings, streets, and parks. The bus dropped us off at a nearby hotel, where we checked into a nice room and were given dinner. When we entered the hotel room, we immediately opened the window to see the sights of freedom, on September 25, 1991. We had closed our home windows in Iraq on November 9, 1990, and had escaped oppression. We were tired, and slept soundly the entire night.

On September 26, we awoke and saw a box of chicken sitting on a table. We were so happy, but then we thought about our big family in Kirkuk and the way in which they were still living under the brutal Saddam, and the thought saddened us. Later that morning, the immigration officer told us to get ready, and we boarded a bus and traveled to a smaller airport, to continue our journey.

Ch. 20- On to the Midwest

Minneapolis Airport and Minot City in North Dakota

On September 26, 1991, we left New York, and after a seemingly short flight we landed in Minneapolis. This time we had no immigration officer with us, and our refugee tags were pinned to our chests. I had trouble finding the right gate. I asked for directions, but my English was still not very good. I looked around for a men's room, and my family warned me not to make the mistake I had made in New York, where I accidentally entered a women's restroom. We finally found the right gate and took off for Minot, North Dakota. The flight attendants learned that we were refugees and were very helpful.

We reached Minot and exited the plane on the runway. My wife asked me, "Where should we go on this huge field?" I told her we would follow the other passengers, and we joined a line that was headed toward the terminal. We arrived and were surprised to see a large group of people waiting for us with a warm greeting. "Welcome Mr. Muhammad's family to America." I thought, "Oh my God, what has happened to us!"We were thrilled and excited. We had reached our goal; we had found the great people in America. The women presented my wife with a bouquet of flowers, and both men and women shook our hands. Television and newspaper reporters were also on hand, recording our arrival.

227

I thought about our experience in Turkey and about the contrast with this American greeting. It was all hard to believe. We joined a long line of fine cars, quite a contrast to the Turkish open, dusty, military trucks that had taken us like cows to die. We drove to downtown Minot and stopped in front of an apartment building. We entered, and the good people of Minot showed us the nice rooms, the furniture, the food in the refrigerator, the sodas and fruits. No more beatings and jails and sleeping on bloody beds covered with insects. Our sponsors said goodnight and left, and we all went to bed, to get some needed rest, but we got little rest. Our Deadly Road nightmare in Turkey was still with us, even in our dreams.

Taha's remarkable dream

Dear reader let me tell you about a dream I had several years before our escape from Kirkuk.

On a dark night, my brother Abbas and I had left Kirkuk. We were walking on highlands and in valleys, guided by an oil lantern. We were silent, and we were sad. We feared capture by Saddam's executioners. I was planning to escape from Iraq, and I knew I would miss my brother Abbas, and it saddened me.

We stood silently on a hill, and I saw a long yellow bright dusty road that extended to a hut that sat among trees. The road seemed covered by yellow gold powder. The hut had a round window that shone like a full moon. My brother stayed in his place, and I started walking toward the hut on the golden road. Everything else around the road was dark.

I got to an area in the upland that was covered with snow. I approached a building, which was a café with huge glass windows, large lights in the front, and electrical outlets. An American flag flew from a pole. The night was still, but the snow on the ground seemed to light the way. I opened the glass entry door, and I saw beautiful plastic chairs and tables.

Before I sit could sit down and drink tea or eat ice cream, I awoke from the dream, and for a moment I saw myself lying on my bed in Iraq awaiting slaughter, as though I were a chicken in a cage, awaiting Saddam's executioner.

I think the dream was a message from Almighty God, telling me that I must take my family to America, and telling me that we would arrive safely in the ice city of Minot, in September of 1991. If I had known that the dream would come true, I wouldn't have been so angry about the betrayal of the smuggler Hussein Saleh, and the treachery of Rashid Agha, and the behavior of the unjust Turkish Muslims on my Long Road to Freedom.

Invitation from Department of Defense
One day, while in Minot, North Dakota, I received an invitation from the US Department of Defense inviting me to attend a ceremony for Colonel James Jones, who was about to be promoted to the rank of general. I had insufficient travel money, and was

unable to attend. This was a disappointment to me and to my family members. He had given us so much help.

Long road to freedom

On the morning of September 27, 1991, we awoke, looked at one another, and then I said, "Yesterday we were homeless, but today we are here in America, living like a normal family."

My wife, Malika, said, "A million times thanks to God and America that we have safely traveled the Long Road to Freedom, which took us from Kirkuk to Minot."

We thought about how far we had come. We had survived racist attacks in Kirkuk by the dictators Abdulkareem Qasim, Abdulsalaam Arif, Abdulrahmaan Arif, Ahmad Hasan Al-Baker, and Saddam. We had survived, except for my oldest son, Lukman, who was killed by a Ba'ath taxi car on June 1, 1981. His death filled our hearts with sadness, but we knew at the time that life had to continue.

We were able to get to Turkey, but were given wrong information by Ghazi in Istanbul and his brother Hussein Salih, the smuggler in Kirkuk, who said that he would help us get to America. His real plan was to turn us over to Saddam, and he almost did on November 17, 1990. God saved us from the Turks, and we followed the road to freedom, which took us to the Zakho camp. God helped us meet Colonel James Jones, who helped us get to Ankara, but we were unable to obtain visas there.

Then the American embassy granted us permission to go to America. In America we no longer had to endure pain—or fire, or snakes, or dangerous animals. God had helped us reach the end of our road to freedom.

While we were enjoying our first breakfast in America, our sponsor arrived and took us to a church, where he introduced us to other parishioners, and to the pastor, a wonderful man. We gradually became familiar with the city of Minot, and we completed the paper work for our social security cards.

A few weeks later, I asked a person from the church to help me call my childhood friend W.S. in Chicago, but the number had been disconnected. I then asked for help in calling another friend, Shawkat, in Los Angeles. His mother answered the phone, and she told me that Shawkat was not at home at the moment, but W.S. was there, and she put him on the phone. I said, "Where is my money, the $2,100?"

He said "What money?" He added that his wife had divorced him and taken all that he had.

I said, "Do you know why this happened to you? I trusted you, but you did not trust yourself and you took my money, and God punished you." I hung up the phone and returned to my family and told them about the call.

After six months of help from the church, my sons found employment at a McDonald's restaurant. Minot was a cold city, with a long winter, and we wanted to move to California. Our friend, Dr. Hoffman, from the church (age 92) had been helping me and my sons with the English language. He called a Kurdish man (Ramadan Zakholy) in California and asked if he could help us find an apartment in San Diego. Ramadan Zakholy gave us the name of another Kurd to contact, a man by the name of Sirajaddeen, and I called him to see if he could help. He said he could, and told me that an apartment in San Diego would be available November 1, 1992.

I informed my landlord in Minot that we would be leaving. I bought airline tickets for six, got rid of all winter clothing, cancelled the utility accounts, gave away much furniture, packed up our few belongings, and prepared to leave Minot. On the morning that we were expecting to leave, the Kurdish man, Sirajaddeen, in San Diego, called and said, "Are you still planning on coming to San Diego?" I told him we were, and that we were going to leave Minot at 8:00 a.m. the next day. He then told me that the apartment we had expected to occupy had been rented to another individual and was no longer available. I was shocked, but thanked him for his help, and hung up the phone.

My family gathered around me and asked me what had happened, and I conveyed the bad news. We had lost the cost of the airline tickets and had lost our winter clothes. I called the landlord the next day, and we were able to keep our apartment, and our utility services. And so in April of 1991, we started our life again, with few possessions. My sons continued to work at

McDonalds, and I found work at a coat factory. We had some dollars, and we bought a used car. I taught my sons how to drive, and we all obtained driver's licenses.

In January of 1992, my wife Malika began having fainting spells, similar to the ones she had experienced in Turkey, when our lives had been periodically threatened. We saw a doctor and learned that Malika had diabetes. The doctor recommended that she stop eating sweets, and told her to avoid sugar and to consume fewer carbohydrates. We all decided to stop consuming sugar, as a way of supporting Malika.

Minot State University

In December 1992, I lost my job at the coat factory, but some co-workers gave me some advice. They said, "You were a math teacher in Iraq. Please, look into attending college in Minot. You can get a degree, and you can teach math in American schools."

I said, "How can I go to college? I have no certificate with me to prove my education?"

They asked, "Why do you not have any certificate with you?"

I said, "On November 9, 1990, the escape day, a smuggler (Rasheed Agha) stole my college certificate at the cold river between Iraq and Turkey."

On January 6, 1993, my oldest son, Yousif, and I went over to Minot State University, and I met with Dr.

Holmen, the chair of the mathematics and computer science department. I had no college certificate, but he worked on my case, and he gave me some math tests, which gave me an opportunity to demonstrate my knowledge. I then began taking math, English, computer, and history classes at Minot State University.

My son, Yousif, also enrolled and began taking pre-medicine courses. My second son, Cameron enlisted in the U.S. Army.

My Son Cameron enlisted in US Army 1993

My third son started eleventh grade at Minot high school, and my youngest son, Rezgar, started seventh grade at the middle school. My wife, Malika, decided to

234

stay at home and attend to the family there, and we were so happy to have her help.

On Friday, March 20, 1993, I got a phone call at 3:00 p.m. at our house. It was a Mrs. Berywan Ali, the wife of our dear friend, Mr. Abdullah Ali. She said, "Come to our home in Bismarck, and on Saturday we will go together to Fargo to attend a Nawroz party, the Kurdish National feast. I immediately accepted her invitation, and we made plans to go to Bismarck.

On that same day, at 4:00 p.m., my wife and my two sons, Rizgar and Saman, and I loaded the car with some simple clothes and hit the road to Bismarck. It was an overcast day, and it was cold, but we placed our trust in God, and we were looking forward to seeing our friends Mr. Abdullah Ali and his family—and to attending a Nawroz party. It was our first trip out of Minot.

Unfortunately, our joy did not last long. Somewhere down the highway I heard a noise, and I thought a stone had hit the car, but I kept driving. The temperature, however, inside the car began to fall; we had lost the heater. My wife said, "Please Taha, increase the heat in the car," I told her it was turned up to high, but the heater was not working. I said I will speed up and try get to Bismarck as quickly as possible.

The cold increased. We had no blankets, and we began shivering. I could feel the cold air coming up my right leg. I could not move my foot because it was on the gas pedal. My wife and children were moving their arms and legs, trying to stay warm. Then frost and ice began covering the windshield, and I could not see the road. I pulled the car over to the shoulder of the road and started the emergency lights, and began scraping ice off the windshield. This cleared the windshield only for a short time, and then I would have to stop and scrape again.

We finally arrived at Abdulla Ali's house. They welcomed us, and we told them what had happened to us in the car. They were amazed that we had arrived safely, since we had no winter travel gear and no cell phone. We all thanked God for helping us escape the cold and potential disaster. The next day we took the car to a mechanic, and for fifty dollars we were able to get the heater fixed. Both families then traveled to Fargo to enjoy the Newroz celebration.

We stayed one night at Mr. Nasrat Hasan's house in Fargo. The next day both families (Mr. Ali's family and my family) returned to Bismarck, and that evening my family and I returned to Minot. But again, it was not an easy drive. A snow storm set in, and I could barely see the road. I was able to follow the car ahead of me, and we finally made it home. But our first trip turned into quite an adventure.

We were slowly beginning to understand American culture. We made friends, Americans and Muslims, and became acquainted with Mike Nygard and his wife, Linda. Mike was a pastor, and for a few months I taught him Arabic. He went to Africa and stayed for

236

many years, working as a pastor. We also became close friends with a woman from the church by the name of Elda. She was 75 years old, and she tried to find a job for me in Minot. Despite all the language and cultural differences, I kept moving forward, working to get my education degree.

I continued to drive my old car, which took me to the University and helped me visit Kurds in Bismarck and Fargo, but it gave me worries. The "Check Engine" light seemed always to be on, and I feared the icy roads. I had no cell phone, so was unable to call 911 in case of an emergency. Malika and I many times cancelled plans to visit others, simply because we worried about the car stalling on the highway. I finally consulted a mechanic, and he told me that the engine was ruined, and it would cost $3,000 to repair it. At that point I had about $300 in my pocket. I returned home, my eyes glued to the "Check Engine" light. The car continued to run well, transporting me to my destinations, which included Minot State University.

We were so happy to be in America, but our hearts would become saddened when we thought about our big families in Kirkuk. We could not talk to them; it would have created a big problem. I was sending my tax return refunds to my wife's family and to my family, delivered by people who were able to travel to Kurdistan, but only to Erbil and Sulaymaniyah. Saddam still controlled Kirkuk.

After we had been in America for three years, I was able to call my big family and I connected with my mom. But she could only make sounds; she was paralyzed and couldn't speak.

I got my equivalent degree in mathematics on August 1, 1994, and I tried to find a teaching job in Minot, but my English was still not very good, so I decided to move to Grand Forks. Dr. Holmen at the University of Minot encouraged me to continue my schooling. Dr. Dawn Rorvig, the great director at the student center office, encouraged me to enroll in the master's degree program at the University of North Dakota, in Grand Forks. She arranged schooling for my sons and me, and helped us find a rented apartment in Grand Forks. We rented a U-Haul truck, and we moved to Grand Forks, North Dakota.

Ch. 21- On to Grand Forks

The University of North Dakota

On August 1, 1994, we loaded our belongings into a U-Haul truck and began our one-day journey to Grand Forks. A rented apartment awaited us, but I didn't know the location; after asking several citizens for directions we finally found it.

We had formulated a plan. My two sons would attend the University of North Dakota and work toward their bachelor's degrees. I would enroll in the same university and pursue a master's degree. I had taken out a $20,000 student loan to get me started, and I was hoping to have enough money to also help my family in Kurdistan.

As I contemplated our financial situation, I received what seemed to be sensational news. A company called Publishers' Clearing House sent me a letter and led me to believe that I had won $10,000,000. The company asked me which outlet I wanted to use to announce this award—personal interview, TV, radio, or newspaper. I was asked first to purchase a $60 gold ring, and I immediately complied. My wife, Malika, and I were thrilled, and we began making plans to bring our relatives to America, and we looked forward to soon becoming wealthy.

I wrote a letter to Publishers' Clearing House thanking them for this prize, and I noted that Jesus must have guided them to Mr. Muhammad. How else would

239

they have known that I needed this money to repay my student loan and to help my family members in America and in Kurdistan?

We waited for a month, as my blood pressure went up, and Malika's blood sugar level increased. I dreamed that I was a millionaire, and I lost hours of sleep. I finally grew tired of waiting, and I went to a health clinic to get some free samples of medication, since I could not afford to purchase the needed meds. I became well, but when I learned that I had been deceived, that there was no $10,000,000 prize, I became sick again. I had also received the sad news that my mother had died in Kirkuk. I had been unable to help her, and I remained a poor student.

Garbage area and furniture
While a student at the University of North Dakota, I met an Iraqi Arab professor who told me that people sometimes discarded old but usable furniture and that this furniture could occasionally be found at the apartment garbage area. One day I looked out our third floor window and spotted a nice, shiny table. I said to Malika and my sons, "I am going to get that table and bring it to our apartment."

They said, "Don't do that."

I told them, "I am a student without income, and that table will help me study my math books."

I walked down to the garbage area, but before I reached it, a new Honda car stopped right next to the table, and a well-dressed gentleman stepped out and said, "Excuse me, sir. Would you give me a hand?" I said I would, and we carefully placed my dream table in his car, and away he went. I looked up at our third floor window, and my wife and sons were waving at me and laughing. I climbed the stairs, disappointed, and slowly entered my poor apartment. But my nice family celebrated the fact that I was not able to get my hands on that table. I said to them, "God made me go there in order to help that rich man."

Master's degree in mathematics

On December 20, 1995, I graduated from the University of North Dakota with a master's degree in mathematics. I did not attend the graduation ceremony; I did not have the kind of clothing I needed for that event, and I could not afford to buy new clothes.

I began searching for a teaching job, or some related kind of job, but I ran into disappointment. I just couldn't find anything. Then six months after graduation, I began receiving letter after letter from the student loan office, asking for repayment of the student loan.

I bought new tires and a new battery for my old car, and I visited many places in North Dakota, looking for employment. One day my car began making a terrible sound; it sounded like someone was beating it with a hammer. I couldn't repair it, and I sold it to a

241

mechanic for $25.00. I then had to depend on friends for transportation.

I was using the internet in my job search, and one day a woman, a school principal, called me from San Francisco, California, and asked me when I could interview for a job. I said, "I have no car, and I am a long way from San Francisco." She told me to come by airplane. I said, "I have no money. I am on the food stamp program. Can you please interview me by phone?" She said no, and immediately hung up the phone.

My heroic wife, Malika, said to me, "Don't worry. You did a good job getting your master's degree, and God will have something for you."

Taha's job search

In early August of 1996, I got a call from a woman by the name of Jeanie, an employee of the Hardin public school district, state of Montana. She asked if I could come to Hardin the next day to interview for a math teaching job. I told her that I did not have a car, and asked if she could conduct a phone interview. She said she would check with the district superintendent and call me back.

My wife and sons gathered around me and asked about the call, and while we were conversing the doorbell rang. My son, Rezgar, opened the door, and there stood a new refugee, Ashraf, a Kurdish friend from Kurdistan. We welcomed him in, and he asked if my

242

oldest son would help him fill out paperwork for the food stamp program. My son said, "I will help you later because my father is waiting for a telephone call about a teaching job in Montana." Ashraf became nervous, like the rest of us, and he stayed to see what would happen.

The telephone rang again, and I picked it up and said, "Hello? Hello?" My son came over and turned the phone right side up. I had been holding it upside down. Again, I said, "Hello," and this time the phone worked. But I was surprised. The voice on the other end did not belong to Jeanie from Hardin. It was Ashraf's wife, and she was crying, and she said, "Brother Taha, my son fell on the cement ground, and his head is bleeding." I stood up, ready to run to Ashraf's house. Everyone asked, "What happened? Why are you confused?" I told them, "Ashraf's wife called, and her son needs help."

Ashraf ran from the room, his papers flying in all directions. Two of my sons followed him, to provide assistance, and I started to follow, but Malika grabbed me and reminded me that the school might be calling me back. I took a seat near the phone, and my lovely wife made me a cup of hot tea. Then the phone rang and I quickly grabbed it, knocking over the cup of tea. I said hello, and the voice said, "Hello, Mr. Muhammad, the district has agreed to do a phone interview. It will be tomorrow at 9:00 a.m." I thanked her, and hung up the phone.

My wife didn't know whether to laugh or cry. I had spilled tea on the nice carpet, but we didn't care. I ran to Ashraf's house, to check on his son and to return his food stamp application papers.

The next morning I got up early to prepare myself for my first telephone interview in America. I took a tablespoon of olive oil to soften my voice, and I took a seat next to the phone, fifteen minutes before the scheduled call. At exactly 9:00 a.m. our phone rang, and the interview commenced, and it seemed to go well. Afterwards, I wiped the sweat from my brow. My wife and sons were proud of the way I had handled the interview, and Malika gave me a glass of orange juice. I began to return to a normal state. But the question remained, "Would the school hire me?"

As we hashed over my responses to the questions, the phone rang again, and this time I handled it in a normal fashion. A voice said, "Hello, Mr. Muhammad. I am the superintendent, and we are offering you a job as a math teacher at Hardin High School. We need you to report on August 16 in order to sign some paperwork. Your salary will be $25,000 per year." I thanked him and told him that I accepted the job. We were thrilled.

Ch. 22- Taha: A Mathematics Teacher in America

Taha travelling to his math teaching job

Following my successful job interview, I decided to travel alone to Hardin, Montana, to follow up on the interview and find a place to reside. I had no car, but my sons lent me theirs, and on August 15, 1996, at 4:00 p.m., I loaded up all my clothes, books, important papers (like college transcripts), and other belongings. Malika prepared some food me, and I as I left, she threw a glass of water toward the rear of the car, a Kurdish custom that is a good luck wish

I arrived in Bismarck in the late evening, and I lost my way among the many unfamiliar streets. I fueled my car and bought a road map, and then called my Kurdish friends, Abdulla Ali and Firyad, whom I had met at the Kurdish Newroz celebration in Fargo, in 1992. Firyad met me, and I followed him to his house, where I joined his family for supper. That evening brother Abdulla and his wife, Barivan stopped by to visit, and they invited me to stay with them that night.

The next morning after breakfast, sister Barivan prepared some "travel food" for me, to nourish me on my trip to Hardin. Abdula Ali showed me the way to Highway I-94 West, and I headed west toward Hardin. I felt good about being on the right road, and I enjoyed the views as I rolled along, but I was also worried, wondering if my old car would make it to Hardin.

245

I stopped for gas near Miles, filled the tank, and consumed the prepared lunch, and then I was approached by some friendly young people who asked about my country of origin. I said I had come from Kurdistan, but they had no idea where that was. I asked them how to get to Hardin, and they showed me the way. They were very helpful.

I got back on I-94 West, and again headed down the road, making progress and enjoying the views. From time to time, however, I would think about my family and worry about my new job in America. I had taught in Kurdistan for twenty-three years, but I didn't know how things would go in America. I then saw the exit to road 47, the path to Hardin, and I said to myself (out loud), "Mr. Muhammad you have made it to Hardin." I looked in the rear view mirror, arranged my hair, and said to myself, "Yes, I will fit into this teaching job." I exited onto 47 and headed toward Hardin.

I finally arrived safely in Hardin and asked for directions to Hardin High School. It was not hard to find it in this small town, and when I entered the school, I was warmly greeted by the principal and several teachers. One teacher then helped me find a house to rent, one close to the school, and I moved in. The house, however, was very old and full of rats and bugs, and it smelled.

The next morning, I decided to take a stroll, and as I walked along, my eyes on the ground, my thoughts wandered back to my family, and I again wondered if

246

my salary would support us. I also wondered if I would be able to help my sons complete their education. While deep in thought, I suddenly saw a huge dog running toward me, but the owner was able to call it back. I was startled, however, and returned safely to my smelly house.

Sons and U-Haul truck

My sons and I developed telephone communication. They called me that day and said that they had rented a U-Haul truck and were going to deliver kitchen appliances and bedroom furniture from our apartment in Grand Forks. I waited expectantly all day, but they didn't arrive. The next day they showed up with the truck, and I was so glad to see them. We hugged, and tears of joy filled my eyes.

I asked them about the delay, and they said, "We left Grand Forks, and two hours later we ran into a bad storm. We thought it might be a tornado, so we stopped the truck on the shoulder of the road and took cover under a small bridge. After a fifteen-minute interlude, we resumed our trip to Bismarck. Unfortunately, however, the truck broke down before we got there. We didn't know what to do, and then an expensive looking car stopped, and the driver offered us a ride to the U-Haul office in Bismarck. Americans always seem ready to help. We reached the U-Haul rental office and explained our problem. The U-Haul manager directed us to a hotel and promised to bring the truck to us the next morning, after the repairs had been made."

After listening to their explanation, I helped unload the appliances and furniture, but I had no way to prepare a meal, or even make tea. They dropped off the U-Haul truck at the rental office. I had followed them there in my car, and I drove them back to Hardin. They then took my car back to Grand Forks, since I was close to the school and had no need for it.

The chair of the Hardin High math department was a man by the name of Arlo Manfull, and I was very fortunate to have him as my leader. He enrolled me in a modern math training class at Billings High School, about forty-five miles away. It was conducted during the summer months, and when I finished that training, my principal gave me a classroom, and I moved in, arranging my desk and computer, on which I kept track of attendance and grades. I prepared my syllabus and printed some classroom rules and policies—and I was good to go, to begin teaching modern math in America.

First year of teaching at Hardin High School
The school year began on August 21, 1996, and I met my first class of thirty students, a real mix, white kids and American Indians, boys and girls. I welcomed them, introduced myself, and gave each student a syllabus. I realized that my accent was difficult for them, so I wrote important points on the blackboard. I had five classes of thirty kids each, a big load.

I didn't have a car, and no way to get to Grand Forks to move Malika to Hardin. So a couple of weeks after the start of the school year, Mr. Arlo Manfull lent me one of his two cars, and on a Friday I headed east on I-94, nearly hitting a deer as I approached Miles. I exited at Miles, filled the gas tank, and picked up a sandwich. Night had fallen, and I resumed my journey. I passed a police car, and suddenly, I saw flashing lights behind me. I pulled over, and the patrolman approached and said, "You were speeding."

I said, "But there is no speed limit in Montana."

He replied, "There is no speed limit during the day, but there is at night."

I told him I had been in Montana for only three weeks, and that I was a high school teacher in Hardin, and this my first experience with night driving. He was very courteous and just gave me a warning ticket, and told me to read the Montana driving regulations.

I reached North Dakota, and as I drove along I thought about the long-ago conflicts between American soldiers and American Indians. I imagined that the spirit of the American Indian was present, standing on a hill or behind a tree, and I imagined that I might be the target of a spear or an arrow. I dismissed this fantasy from my mind, and again focused on my driving. But then I again began to imagine Indians on horseback behind my car, or waiting for me around the curve in the road. I knew the source of these fantasies. I had taken an American history class at Minot State University, and I had acquired some knowledge of Native American history.

The bright lights of a gas station brought me back to reality, and I pulled off the highway to get gas. I also bought some water and potato chips, and again headed toward Grand Forks. I arrived at about midnight. I did not have a cell phone, so I was not able to let family members know I was home. I knocked softly on the door, and a voice said, "Who is it?"

I said, "It is Taha, your dad."

My sons opened the door and hugged me, as did Malika—they were so happy to see me. I stayed for two days, and then Malika came back with me to Hardin. She was very happy to join me and happy to see that I was successfully employed. After a month in the old house, we rented a nice apartment, and several months later I was able to buy a used car, so that we could visit our sons in Grand Forks.

In Hardin, I learned to go to the grocery market, use the post office, and travel to Billings, where I would often visit the auto repair shop. I also continued taking math courses there, to improve my teaching skills.

Malika and I had wanted to become American citizens, and one day we drove to the Montana capital, Helena, and took the citizenship test. We did well, and a few months later we reported to the Billings courthouse for a citizenship ceremony. On May 8, 1997, a judge declared that we were US citizens, and it was a happy day. When we returned to Hardin, we decided to celebrate, and we invited our landlord and a few teachers

250

over to enjoy some Iraqi food. A few weeks later we obtained American passports.

My second year at Hardin High School

On August 20, 1997, I started my second year at Hardin High, this time with the aid of an assistant, Mr. Peace. Everything was going well at school, and my sons were pursuing their education at the University of North Dakota. I was able to financially support them. I worried, however, about our big family in Kurdistan—they were struggling with the bad economic conditions.

In October of 1997, the school gave me a two-week leave (without pay) to visit Malika's seriously ill brother in Kurdistan. We flew to Istanbul, where Turkish security people delayed our trip to Diyarbakir. They ordered us to fly to Ankara. On the plane, we felt like semi-hostages. We arrived, and made our way to the terminal's waiting area, but then Turkish security officials separated us from the other passengers, and began to closely inspect our passports. Thank God we had American passports; otherwise, we might have been jailed, the way we were jailed from November 10, 1990, to April 24, 1991—when we were refugees in Turkey.

Turkish officials finished checking us out, and I asked them why they had directed us to Ankara instead of Diyarbakir, and why they had taken our American passports. One official said, "We thought you were bringing a lot of goods to sell in Turkey". That answer made no sense.

251

We were finally escorted to the plane that would take us to Diyarbakir, but our tickets had been confiscated. Nonetheless, officials allowed us to board the plane, and we took our seats. A passenger next to us began asking question after question, all the way to the Diyarbakir airport. He did not know that I knew he was a civilian security agent. He recommended that we stay at a certain hotel in Diyarbakir, but I ignored that suggestion. We landed in Diyarbakir, and I then tried to retrieve our bags, but they had disappeared.

Nighttime had come, and Malika and I were confused. Where were our bags? Then a Kurdish taxi driver from the Kurdish area of Turkey spotted us and said to me, "Come here, uncle, your bags are in my car." He agreed to take us to the Kurdish part of Iraq, and he informed us that the road from Diyarbakir to Kurdistan was dangerous at night. He did not say why, but I knew why. There were Kurdish freedom fighters along the way, Kurds who had been fighting for independence and rights since 1984. Turks had named these Kurds "Mountain Turks" in an attempt to erase their identity. The driver recommended that we stay in a hotel that night and then continue by car to Kurdistan. We agreed on that plan.

Early the next morning we rejoined the taxi driver and set out for Iraqi Kurdistan. As we rolled along, we noticed the differences between the Kurdish areas of Turkey and the conditions in Ankara and Istanbul. The Kurds were obviously poor, even though

Kurdistan itself was rich in resources. We also recalled our suffering in Turkey in the years 1990 and 1991.

We arrived at the Kurdistan part of Iraq, an area that Americans had declared a no-fly zone, and I saw the ways in which two Kurdish leaders, Masud Barzani and Jalal Talabani, had brought improvements to the Kurdish region. They had helped establish schools, colleges, parks, and modern buildings. They had addressed human rights issues, and had worked to extend rights to women and children. But the news about our big families was sad. Both of our mothers had died, and many relatives had been killed by Saddam's forces. One female relative, Fawzia (age 56) had been shot and killed by a helicopter, along with her daughter (22) and her son (25).

Malika and I stayed for nine days and then returned to Hardin, where we were warmly welcomed by students and teachers. They asked all about our trip, and I expressed my appreciation for the ways in which America was helping and protecting Kurdish people, forcing the criminal and dictator Saddam to halt the killing of the peace-loving Kurdish people. I was very happy to resume my teaching.

Turkey intelligence at my school
A few weeks after our return, a group of Turks came to my school and met with students and teachers— but not with me. My assistant, Mr. Peace, an American Indian from the Crow reservation, told me about the meeting. The Turks had tried to place blame on the Kurds, and to portray themselves as victims of Turkish

Kurds. They lied. They did not inform these Americans that Turks had oppressed Kurds for decades, going all the way back to 1915. I said to Mr. Peace, "Someday God will help Kurdistan. He will punish those who have killed and tortured Kurds. And someday the sun will shine over Kurdistan's land, and the Kurds will find peace and enjoy basic human rights."

In 1997, Malika had been told by a doctor, after a mammogram screening, that she had cancer in her breast. We did not tell our sons in Grand Forks, North Dakota, but the news hit me hard. I did not show my sadness to Malika. I wanted to keep her strong to let her know that God was protecting her.

Fortunately, the surgery was successful, and the hospital in Billings informed us that Malika was cancer free. When I received this news, I felt like I could fly like a bird around the world and gather the world's nicest flowers to give to her, to recognize her return to good health

About midway through the school year, I made plans to bring my sons to Hardin, but the landlord informed me that I could not move them into my apartment; it was rented to accommodate only me and Malika. On January, 1, 1998, we moved to a house in Billings, and I commuted to Hardin each day—a 45-mile, one-way trip. The road was dangerous in the winter, but I had to continue my teaching job, while providing housing for my family. In June of 1998, I bought a nice house, with a front and back yard.

Anyway, I successfully completed my second and third years at Hardin High School, and I then took a minimum wage job at the IGA grocery store, while I looked for another teaching job. My supervisor was one of the most respectful individuals I have ever met. He was helpful to everyone, and I used the job services in Billings to help me in my job search. I also contacted my childhood friend Shawkat, in Los Angeles, to discuss my ambitions and needs.

Ch. 23- Taha's Search for a Job in Los Angeles

Visit to Los Angeles

In July of 1999, I was invited to visit my childhood friend, Shawkat Yahya Ezrumly, in Los Angeles, and so I decided to take a Greyhound bus from Billings to L.A., to look for employment. I stayed for a week, but found nothing; and then I took a Greyhound bus to Billoings, Montana. The bus dropped us at midnight at a Greyhound bus station in Las Vegas, Nevada, and I did enjoy the bright lights there. I finally caught a bus at 1:00 a.m. back to Billings.

The bus stopped at certain points for coffee and restroom, and at one stop I visited a restroom, ordered a cup of coffee, came out of the store, and saw the bus disappearing down the highway. I ran after it, to no avail, then grabbed a rock and threw it at the bus, but I didn't come close. That bus was gone.

I returned to the store to see if I could find help. One gentleman in a pickup truck had seen my predicament, and he beckoned me over and said that he would help me catch up with the bus. We took off, exceeding the speed limit, and finally caught up. My friend, the pickup driver, waved the bus over to the shoulder, and I was able to back get on board. I was a bit angry at the bus driver for leaving me behind, but I found my travel bag and took a seat. I took a book from my bag, but I was unable to read. I kept looking at the scenic American landscape, as we rolled along. The bus

256

continued to stop from time to time, and I always told the bus driver to wait for me while I used the restroom.

I finally arrived in Billings, and my family seemed disappointed that I had been unable to land a job But they were glad to see me. The job service office in Billings continued to help me. They covered travel and interview expenses, and they paid for a trip to Texas, to interview for a teaching job. They also provided financial to help me attend a math teaching job fair in Grand Forks. They also helped with mortgage payments and spending money.

Taha's trip to Minnesota

On August 16, 1999, the Minneapolis public school district called to tell me I had been hired to teach math at Roosevelt High School in Minneapolis, Minnesota. My new salary would be $65,000 instead of the $32,000 I had received at Hardin High School. At the time, I was driving a car I had previously been using, because I had given my other car to my sons.

On that same day, I drove from Billings to Minneapolis, but the car had developed some kind of engine problem, and I was able to drive only thirty miles per hour. It was nighttime, and I had no access to a car repair service and no cell phone with which to call AAA.

I came to a small town near Jamestown, North Dakota about 12:20 a.m. and drove to the downtown area, looking for someone who could direct me to a police station or to a motel. One friendly gentleman informed me that the town has no police force or motels. I asked if he would use my Triple-A card to call an 800 number and see if I could have my car towed to Fargo for repair. He told me to follow his car, and we stopped at a garage, but it was closed. We found a wall phone, however, and I gave him my Triple A card, and he called them. A truck came and towed my car to Fargo, arriving at 3:24 a.m. A mechanic fixed my car that morning, and he wanted to replace all the defective parts. I tried to dissuade him, but he went ahead, and I wound up with a $600 bill, which I paid with a credit card. I hadn't expected that kind of bill. Nonetheless, I was happy. I knew I would not be late for my interview in Minneapolis, and that I would be able to complete all the paperwork.

I arrived in Minnesota, but lost my way several times in Minneapolis. I finally met my son in Edina, a suburb. He had come a week earlier; the University of Minnesota had accepted him into its chiropractic program. On August 18, he helped me find the Minneapolis school district office, and I met with Carol at the human resources department, and signed the teaching contract. She gave me a copy of the contract, which verified my income and which allowed me to rent an apartment in Eagan, a thirty-mile drive from my school.

On August 19, I returned to Billings and rented a U-Haul. The Montana job service people gave me $1,000 for the U-Haul rental and $1,200 for the first month's rent. I gave a realtor in Billings power of attorney to sell my house, so I could pay off the mortgage and maintain my good credit rating.

On August 20, my family members, neighbors, and Kurdish friends helped load my belongings into my car and into the U-Haul; and Malika and I left Billings, as all the neighbors waved goodbye. But suddenly the truck began to shake, and I turned off the engine to see what was wrong. The neighbors ran to the truck, and one friend determined that shift number 1 was not working, and that I would have to drive with shift number 2. I made it to Interstate Highway 94 East, but remained very nervous. The car could go only 65 mph, and other trucks kept passing us. We were afraid that we would arrive at night, and I would not be able to find my way.

The gas gauge showed the tank half empty, so I turned off at an exit to find a gas station. I got stuck at the gas station; I did not know how to maneuver the long truck to the right pump, and cars began backing up behind me. Finally, two or three gentlemen came to my assistance. They got me to the right spot, and rescued me and got me out of a difficult situation. I thanked them profusely.

We felt good about the new job in Minnesota, but the defective truck was making us unhappy. Night came, and we were still on the road. I found another gas station and filled the tank. When I backed up, however, the truck hit the trailer, making a loud sound. Several truck drivers came to my assistance and signaled with their hands how I should correctly turn the steering wheel. We finally made it to Minnesota, but with a few slight damages to the truck and trailer.

After some difficulty, we found our apartment in Eagan, after driving for twenty hours. It was 4:00 a.m., but my son, Yousif, was at the apartment waiting for us. We were so tired; we fell asleep on the carpeted floor and slept until 9:00 that evening.

First school year (1999-2000)
On August 23, I began my teaching duties at Roosevelt High School. My classes contained white and black students, one Somali student, and several Asian students. The Somali students at the school saw me as a big brother, and even a father figure. The other American students all welcomed me and showed great respect. On my first day, some students wanted to do negative things in the classroom, but other students stopped them.

The three-story school building held 1,700 students, and the principal, Fred Meyer, placed me with the Math Club Team and Teachers Leadership Team. It was cool for me to be in this school. I attended several teacher education courses, and I got involved with many school activities. The teachers were very friendly and helpful, especially Mr. Ivan Geffert. Teachers invited my wife and me to their houses, and we invited them to ours. I volunteered to teach on Saturdays, the only teacher who volunteered. The principal appreciated my efforts, and he wrote a letter describing my work with the students and expressing his gratitude.

I had sold my house in Billings, and in February of 2000, I bought a house in Lakeville. I attended a summer school course for teachers, and on July 15, Malika and I traveled to Sweden to visit my sister-in-law, a refugee in that country. We enjoyed our time in Sweden, and on August 16 we returned to our lovely house in Lakeville with gifts for our sons.

Second school year (2000-2001)

My second year began well. I had great students and an excellent principal, Mr. Fred Meyer. I attended the usual teacher education classes, and I again volunteered to teach on Saturdays. I completed the second year, and I received congratulations from both the students and parents, who appreciated my work. They wrote nice letters to me, thanking me for helping their sons and daughters. I attended summer school sessions, and I bought a new car. Our school principal retired, however, and we got a new principal for the upcoming school year.

Third school year (2001-2002)

I started my third year at Roosevelt High, this time with a new car, and no fear of stalling on the road from Lakeville to the school. I had many students in my math classes, and everything seemed to be going well. And then on September 11, 2001, tragedy hit.

On that day, after a second period class, I went to the cafeteria for a cup of coffee. The female math teacher entered the room, and she looked very sad. She said, "Mr. Muhammad, what is going on!" Her voice

261

indicated something bad had happened, but I had no idea what she was talking about.

I put my coffee down and said, "What is it?

She then told me planes had crashed into the Twin Towers in New York and into the Pentagon building, and then she quickly left the cafeteria. I ran to my classroom and called Malika. She was crying, and said she had locked our doors and piled up chairs behind the main door. She said, "I'm afraid for you and our sons. Are you OK?"

I didn't know what to think. I was confused and upset. I wanted to learn more. Why was my wife locking doors, piling up chairs, worried about me and our sons? I was trying to maintain control of myself. I said to Malika, "Please, would you let me know what the problem is?"

She said, "The world is done, everything will be nothing, and all will die."

My brain ordered my heart to beat even faster, and I put my left hand to my head, while still holding the phone. I wanted to hang up, but in my culture that would have been disrespectful, so I waited until she could give me a description of the problem. Terrorists had attacked the World Trade Center in New York and destroyed the buildings, and killed about 3,000 Americans.

I could hardly speak. Every system in my body seemed like it was about to stop. My free period passed, and my students came in for the third period class. I was not prepared for them. I had a bad feeling that bad things were going to happen from this day forward.

Cautions and fears

I made it through the day, but I don't know how, and I drove home in a very sad state of mind. I almost hit another car, and the driver became very angry. He swore at me and gave me the finger sign. He may have said, "In New York, planes attack, and in Minnesota cars attack." The driver had a right to be a little angry. I was emotionally upset, and I came too close to his car. I gained control of myself and apologized, but I don't think he heard me. I continued driving, hoping that Americans would understand that we were Kurds—and that we were victims in Iraq, like the Armenians in Turkey and the Jews in Germany had been victims.

After the 9-11 tragedy

I arrived home, and my wife hugged me. Her tears spilled onto me, and I could see that she was pale. I calmed her down and told her there was nothing to fear, because we were not in any way associated with the attackers. We sat around the TV, and I learned that the World Trade Center had been attacked by Muslims. We prayed for the safety of all Americans. We were sure Americans would obey the law and would not see us as people who were allied with the attackers.

The next day at school, I climbed the stairs to my third floor room, moving like a 90-year-old man, and I began teaching. But I could see that some students were troubled. They knew I was a Muslim, but they did not know that I was a Kurd, and that our family and many others had been persecuted. I wanted to tell them that I had nothing to do with this tragedy.

As usual, I volunteered to teach Saturday school, for which I did not receive or expect payment. I attended the usual education classes, and I successfully completed the three-year probationary period. The school district decided that I had earned tenure, and they gave me a $1,000 gift.

The tenure decision was very important to my family. It allowed us to stay in house, in one state—and to keep our friends. I intended to go forward and to start my fourth year, and then on September 14, 2002, I was offered another job. I was asked to work as a translator for American military troops in Kuwait and Iraq.

Ch. 24- Taha: Military Linguist in Iraq

Linguist for US military forces

I accepted employment with the Titan Systems Corporation, a civilian company in Virginia that provided various forms of assistance to US military forces, and I began my service as a linguist for the American forces In Kuwait and Iraq. I was motivated to serve because of my deeply felt desire to help topple the dictator Saddam.

I began my service in Virginia and then moved to Columbus, Georgia, home of a military training and deploying base. While there, I learned the term "chow hall" (military restaurant). I slept on the top part of a bunk bed, but bothered the soldier on the bottom part with my restless turning that shook the entire bunk. On the first night, when I went to take a shower, I saw two naked men in the shower, I couldn't bring myself to shower with them, and I returned at midnight to shower in privacy.

The next day I told an Afghani linguist about the shower problem, and he just laughed at me. He said, "Try it just one time, and then it will be normal forever." But I could not shower with other men, and I don't know how the Afghani man was able to do so.

I completed training with the civilian company CRC, and on December 29, 2002, I was transported to Arefjan military base in Kuwait, where I learned to use a gas mask and other measures designed to protect us. I shared a tent with nine other men, and I ate at scheduled times, hungry or not. One tent provided showers; we had ten minutes to take a morning shower. Soldiers waited in a long line for their showers.

Taha Linguist In Kuwait January 2002

I was transferred to a base called Camp Doha to work with Army intelligence personnel. On February 5, 2003, while in training, I jumped from a military vehicle and injured myself, and I was sent back to the US for surgery, which was successful. While waiting to recover, Titan Corporation paid me 60% of my regular salary.

Taha as linguist in Iraq

On July 1, 2003, I took another job with a company in Maryland called All World Languages Consultants. I went directly from there to Kuwait, and then to Balad base in Iraq. The plane dropped off thirty soldiers, and then we flew to Qatar. I was the only passenger. Shortly before landing, the plane developed an engine problem on the left side, and it filled with smoke. We were already over Qatar, however, and we landed safely, but the pilot said, "Hurry Mr. Muhammad, and leave your bags in the plane." I quickly exited and then saw firefighters, ambulances, and camera men rushing toward the plane. It had been a potentially dangerous situation, but it all ended well. I retrieved my bags, and after a three-day wait I flew to Kirkuk, in Kurdistan of Iraq, to assist the US troops. My fluency in English, Arabic, Kurdish, and Turkish was most helpful, and my salary was much greater than my Roosevelt High School salary.

Taha Linguist in Kirkuk/ Iraq

I once had a "near miss"—a potentially life threatening event. While working in the Pass and ID office, a fifty-caliber bullet came through the wall and went through the loose part of my pant leg. God saved

267

me. I had dreamed about my father the previous night. He had died in 1975. In the dream, he tapped me on the right shoulder and asked me to go with him. It was a good dream, because I chose not to go with him.

Fifty-caliber bullet came through the wall

While serving in Iraq, my family sold our house in Lakeville, Minnesota, and rented an apartment in Eagan. We hoped eventually to move to California or Virginia when the time was right.

My wallet and Diyarbakir, June 30, 2004

On June 30, 2004, I planned to return to the US on a vacation. Malika was with me in Kurdistan, and we decided to see some sights, first in Diyarbakir, a Kurdish city, which unfortunately was under Turkish control.

268

One morning on July 1, 2004, on Gazi Street in the city of Diyarbakir, we were viewing the Kurdish King Amid's historic wall, when suddenly I felt a blow to my right side pocket. It came from a strong young man who was attempting to steal my wallet. I thought he had succeeded, and I began chasing him, down one alleyway that divided into two alleyways. I was yelling at him, using words like, "Stop! Otherwise, I will shoot you!"

The poor would-be thief finally held out his open palms and continued running, showing me that he had nothing in his hands. Then I saw that my wallet was hanging from my pant belt, and that had prevented the theft. I had tied my wallet securely to my belt. Inside the wallet were two American passports, $3,000, two airplane tickets to Minnesota, and my American driver's license.

I returned to Malika, to make sure she was OK. We were among many of Diyarbakir's good people, old and young, male and female Kurds. They gathered around us, asking what had happened. While responding to their questions, I was hit again by another thief, who again tried to steal my wallet. He failed, and he ran away like a rat running from a cat. I just laughed at him, and I thought about all the inhumane people I had encountered, and I said to myself, "What would happen if an innocent person were to meet those thieves in a forest?" The Gazi Street was filled with hundreds of people. Then suddenly a third thief ran by me, but without touching my hand. He may have been afraid of me, and for good reason.

My brave wife (Malika) did not faint, as she had in November 1990, March 1991, and April 1991—while we were escaping from Iraq and encountering life threatening dangers in Turkey. Malika said to the people around her, "It is a shame that people attack visitors in their city." Some people around her said the situation in Diyarbakir created thieves, and others said the thieves were not Kurds. The people on the street were very upset and told us, "Please, don't go anymore to Gazi Street, because thieves are always killing visitors for their money, and they are not Kurds. They are Turks, and they have a political goal—to make Kurds look bad.

Mom and dad with sons, July 2, 2004
The next day, July 2, 2004, we flew from Diyarbakir to Istanbul, where the police again searched our bags, but they couldn't detain us—we had American passports. My name, however, was in their computer system, with notes. After a short but stressful time, we flew out and landed safely in Minnesota. We were glad to get back to our apartment, and when I told my sons about our adventure on Gazi Street in Diyarbakir, they laughed and said, "Wherever you go, you wind up with a story to tell." It was great to be back with our sons.

I could see that my family did not want to leave Minnesota, so I decided to buy a house, and I found one in Lakeville, close to my previous Lakeville house. After a ten-day vacation, I returned to Kirkuk, to help our troops and the Iraqi people.

The last six months in Iraq as a linguist, January 14, 2005 to July 15, 2005

Sometime later, I got a three-day leave from the base, and I was able to visit my doctor brother in Sulaymaniyah, a one-hour drive from Kirkuk, going east. It was a safe place for Americans, and I enjoyed the views—mountains, green landscapes, and blue sky. I returned to Kirkuk with gifts for my family in America, and as I started to move through the gate, and return to my base, a strange thing happened.

I was initially warmly greeted; everyone knew me, and I had my military ID pinned to my chest. Suddenly one soldier and was alone at the gate yelled at me, "Stop or I will shoot you." I was about fifty feet from the gate, and I recognized the soldier, and I thought he knew me. It was evening, but it was not dark. I thought he was joking, then I realized he was serious; he was prepared to shoot me.

I said, "I am Mr. Muhammad of the Pass and ID office, and I have been on this base almost two years."

He said, "Don't move, or I will shoot you." I raised my arms and tried to show him my ID, but nothing worked. I said, "What shall I do?"

He told me, "Go back."

I said, "I am here to help the Iraqi people and American troops." He did not respond, and I became confused and frightened. I said to myself, "Mr. Muhammad, this is your final day in this unjust world. This soldier I have met, and he knows Arabic a little bit, but why is he going to kill me?" He kept aiming his machine gun at me. Why did he not approach me, and check my ID? Then an American security agent stepped out of his car, saw the situation, and immediately put himself between me and the sniper.

The agent said, "This is Mr. Muhammad, the famous linguist at this base." The sniper put down his machine gun, and my heart started to calm down. I approached the sniper and asked him, "Why did you want to kill me?"

He said, "I thought you were a terrorist."

I said, "Why did you not look at my DOD ID first, and then decide if I was terrorist or not?"

He replied, "I did not recognize your ID from that far away."

I said, "I recognized you. I met you five days ago at this gate. This gate number three is for people to enter the base under requirements of the base policy! Why did you not use your binoculars that are in front of you to recognize me?"

I began walking toward my room, but I was sweating, although my heart had begun to slow down. I had been close to death, right on the base. Each day more than 1,000 Iraqi workers passed through this gate, and none were ever suspected of being a terrorist. Why me? Who planned this? And why? I had earned great respect from military leaders and soldiers. The event just didn't make sense.

I had completed two years of service in Kirkuk, Iraq, and I was proud to have been part of the effort to topple dictator Saddam. He had used weapons of mass destruction against the Kurds, against Iran's soldiers and civilians, and against Shiites in Iraq. He had also killed hundreds of Sunnis in Ramadee, Baghdad, and Tikreete. He committed terrible atrocities. He once allowed four German dogs to attack and kill Dr. Rajee Al-Tikreety in Saddam's presidential palace.

A Certificate of Security Force

273

On July 10, 2005, I ceased working with the ALC Company and made plans to return to America. Some of my military colleagues, however, told me that the Defense Language Institute in Monterey, California, might be interested in my services, teaching Arabic. The base commander gave me a strong letter of recommendation, and on July 15, 2005, I flew to Qatar from Kirkuk. The colonel who piloted the plane knew me, and he waded through thirty soldiers to greet me. Up in the air, he announced, "Mr. Muhammad is in the airplane with us. We are proud of him. He survived a 50-caliber bullet that passed through his pants."

The military plane arrived at the Qatar airport, and I waited at Camp Doha for two days. I enjoyed those two days, and then I flew to Germany, and after a three-hour stop, flew to Baltimore. I visited my civilian company headquarters, and I gave them my military ID. I then signed some papers stating that I had successfully completed my term of employment.

I traveled to Reagan airport in Washington D.C., and after entering my name in a computer, the woman at the airline counter said, "Wait, please, because one bad person has your same name." She was very polite, but I was disappointed that Americans did not recognize the dangerous mission I had completed on behalf of the US military forces.

I was finally able to get home to my great house in Lakeville, Minnesota. Malika and our heroic sons were all so happy to see me. I had served our new country well, and with distinction.

Ch. 25- Taha: A Math Teacher in CA

Simons Middle School, Oakland, California

On August 26, 2005, the Oakland public school district called, and I did a telephone interview, and they hired me to teach math at Simons Middle School. This was on a Thursday. Malika and I packed four big bags, bought our tickets, and flew out of Minneapolis to San Francisco. I had planned to meet with a member of the human resources office, to get help finding an apartment close to the school, since I didn't have a car. On Friday, I called the number I'd been given, but there was no answer

On Monday I reported to the district office to get apartment help and to sign a contingency contract based on a copy of my transcripts. The clerk took my fingerprints and sent me to a clinic for chest x-ray. I was told to report to the school the next day. I still didn't know my salary, since the school officials were still waiting for my transcripts, and I still didn't have an apartment. I finally found an apartment in Walnut Creek, thirty miles from the school, and I signed a six-month lease. On September 2, I bought a new car, and I reported to the school the next day.

The students had been led by a substitute teacher for ten days, and they were out of control. I treated them well, but they were tough on me. I had no way to instill discipline except to call the parents after school, and even that option was limited, since the phone in my classroom didn't work. There seemed to be about ten troublemakers in each of the six classes, but when I observed them in other classes, they were behaving like angels.

On September 7, 2005, on the third day of my teaching year, students began throwing paper balls at one another. I'd had enough. I immediately resigned and said goodbye to that school. Malika was a little disappointed, but I was able to break my apartment lease, which cost me about $2,000, and we also lost some furniture. We loaded our kitchen materials into our new car, and placed other items in the garbage area, hoping some needy person would find them.

Barber shop and back to Minnesota

On that same day, September 7, we traveled to Sacramento to visit our son, who had temporarily rented a house there. The next day I decided to get a haircut, and the female barber practically turned me into a bald man. I looked like someone who had just escaped from prison. Malika seemed sad, probably for two reasons— my quitting my job and my horrible haircut. But she also thought we should return to Lakeville and apply for a teaching job in the Twin Cities area.

On September 9, 2005, we set out for Minnesota, following Highway 80 East, and reached Salt Lake City, where we rented a motel room. The next day we hit Wyoming, and as we drove along we passed a big truck that began throwing rocks and sand on my lovely new car. A highway patrolman then stopped me, and when he saw that my car was loaded with materials, and that I had a strange haircut, he seemed to become suspicious. He gave me an $80 speeding ticket, the first in my life, and I was 61 at the time.

We continued on our journey, observing the speed limit, but many cars and trucks passed us—they seem unconcerned about the speed limit. I thought to myself, maybe big trucks should be required to move at a slower speed than small vehicles. We reached Nebraska and took a motel room. The next day we reached Iowa and took the familiar I-35 highway north, finally arriving at our nice house in Lakeville, Minnesota.

Ch. 26- Taha's Trip South

A trip to Nashville, October 2005

While working at the US military base in Kirkuk, I formed a friendship with another Kurd linguist, Wouria Shwani, who had settled in Nashville, Tennessee. He called me and talked about some farmland that was for sale, and he asked me to come down and take a look at it. I bought a plane ticket and flew south.

One day before the sale, we visited the site, which was in northern Kentucky, an hour's drive from Nashville. The land sat next to some Amish property, and the Amish farmers and others—about 150 in all—had also come to bid on it. My friend and I had decided to each put up $10,000 for the purchase of twenty acres. We were prepared to pay $2,500 per acre, but the sale, as it turned out, was for four pieces of land valued at $350,000. We had intended to buy a small acreage, build a simple farmhouse, and learn how to farm and raise lambs. But we had to abandon that plan

While there, my friend, Wouria Shwani, and I visited a senior member of the Amish group, Uncle David (the grandpa). I learned from him much about the Amish lifestyle, and I observed the ways in which they dressed and the ways they used their horse drawn buggies. My friend said that each week he purchased from Uncle David and his son eggs, milk, and organic vegetables. Uncle David knew about Kurdistan, and he agreed that it should have statehood, and should be an independent country. I said to him, "Uncle David, you

279

and I have to go to the United Nations office and demand that Kurdistan become a country."

He laughed and said, "Wait, we will pray for God to do that." His answer was logical, and we are both waiting for God to create a separate Kurdistan. As we were about to leave, uncle David said to me, "Move from Minnesota to Nashville and come visit me." Wouria Shwani and I left the sale area without making any purchase. =

While in Nashville, I visited the University of Tennessee human resources office and obtained information about how to apply for a teaching job. After three days in Nashville, we returned to Minnesota.

Mr. Muhammad and All-World Language Consultant again

When I returned to Lakeville, I decided to call my previous employer, the company that had hired me to work as a linguist. The manager said he could place me in Qatar and told me, "You have to complete your security clearance."

I said, "Why? I already have clearance. I worked for ALC for two years in dangerous Iraq."

She said, "I wasn't your manager. I will send you a plane ticket by email today, and you can come here and complete your interview and take a polygraph test. And you can do this on December 26, 2005." She sent me a contract, which stipulated that I would have health insurance and that I would be paid $100 per day until I had completed my security clearance. I flew to Rockville, Maryland, took a hotel room, and reported to ALC the next for my interview and test.

ALC linguist and movie renter thief

Following the polygraph test, an ALC employee dropped me off at my hotel, and a manager called the hotel and told them that I had to arise at 5:00 a.m. the next morning. The company had arranged for a ride to the airport. I began to fall asleep about 8:00 that evening, but then a hotel clerk called and gave me a number to call. I made the call, and the person who answered told me I had a wrong number. I did not mention this to the hotel manager.

I got up early the next morning and went down to check out at the front desk. The clerk handed me a bill for $20. I said, "What is this for?"

He said, "Last night you ordered two movies, and this is your phone number and your call!" I thought maybe the night clerk had concocted this movie plan as a way of making a crooked dollar. But I just decided to pay it; I didn't want to be late for my flight to Minnesota. While traveling to the airport, I described the movie rental problem to the driver. He seemed nervous, and then he lost his way, which was odd, since he had frequently made the trip. I learned that he was waiting for his security clearance, and he told me that a previous translator had paid close to $1,000 for movies he had never ordered.

281

Anyway, as we drove toward the airport, I began to solve the crime. The driver, an ALC linguist, had ordered the movies under my name. Nobody else knew my room number and the room's telephone number except him. He had gotten it by telling the hotel that he was from ALC and that he was giving me a ride to the airport. We finally arrived, and I boarded the plane. But I wondered how this Moroccan could defraud people while working as a translator and holding a top security clearance.

It took three months for ALC to process my security clearance, and I had to call them and email them a hundred times to get the income they had promised. I finally decided to resign, and on June 1, 2006, I applied for employment at the Defense Language Institute (DLI) in Monterey, California. I was prepared to teach Arabic.

Ch. 27- Taha: Teacher at DLI Institute

US Defense Language Institute (DLI), Monterey, California

On June 18, 2006, on the same day I resigned from the ALC linguist company, I was hired by the Defense Language Institute (DLI) in Monterey, California. I called a family friend, Jiin Khaqnaqa in Monterey, and asked if she would find an apartment for us. She did, and I signed the lease by fax, and paid the deposit. The landlord said that the apartment would be available on June 19, 2006. Malika and I loaded up our Honda car and set out, this time hoping that California would be our last stop, God willing.

I began my teaching duties on June 26, and I found the setting and workplace immediately rewarding, for several reasons:

Teachers were from Middle East, Africa, and other parts of the world; and I enjoyed associating with them as colleagues.

I was happy and proud to be associated with my director, an Egyptian.

The students were American military folks, and they took seriously their responsibilities.

The job was a federal civil service appointment, and my rights were protected by law.

283

The Pacific Ocean was a beautiful sight to behold.

When I was introduced to some Arab teachers, they asked where I was from, and I said, "I am from Kurdistan of Iraq." A few Arabs seemed to dislike that fact about me, but I told them that Kurds had rights, and that those rights were being denied by Muslim countries like Iraq, Turkey, Iran, and Syria.

On weekends, I would paint, and I created twelve pieces of art. I had to quit that avocation though. A car hit my car from behind, and I injured my neck, making it impossible to focus on the painting activity. I gave one painting to the dean at Middle East School One, and I gave others to friends.

Taha's Art- the Pacific Ocean

Taha's Art- Imaginary View

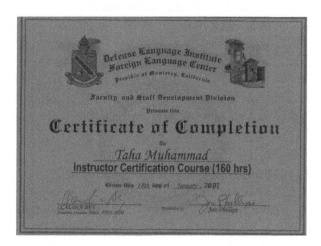

Certificate of US Defense Language Institute

285

I took some vacation time and travel ed to Germany to see my son, who had become engaged. I was thoroughly enjoying my job in Monterey. Malika wanted to visit a diabetes doctor, but we could not find one in Monterey. My son in San Diego found one for us, so I asked the temporary replacement of the director for a leave to visit a clinic in San Diego. She granted permission for the leave, but after two days the principal director attended his office and overruled her, and would not grant the leave.

I then asked to be transferred to another school, and I moved over to the Continuing Education School, with the help of the Institute's dean Dr. Robert. On the day I was to transfer, I received warm hugs and goodbyes from the dean, both secretaries, and the military people. My new dean and manager were both high level professionals.

My job consisted of traveling to military bases and teaching officers the Iraqi dialect. I first traveled to a base in San Antonio, Texas, and taught there for one week—and then returned to Monterrey.

Teaching at Leavenworth base in Kansas
On October 11, 2007, I took a second trip, this time to Leavenworth, Kansas. I taught the Iraqi dialect there for two months. The commander admired my work and awarded me the school coin. I enjoyed teaching the officers. They were all eager to learn.

I returned to Monterey, but I did not like the fog and the cool (below 70 degree) temperature. I applied for a six-month leave without pay, and decided to return to my house in Lakeville. DLI approved the leave request. I said goodbye to some of the Kurdish teachers, and I thanked them for all the help they had given me. Malika and I again loaded up our Honda, and we set out for Lakeville.

Ch. 28- Driving from California to Minnesota

Mr. Muhammad on the road

On December 12, 2007, at 2:00 p.m., I loaded up my 2005 Honda with household and personal items and set out for Sacramento, about a three-hour drive from Monterey. I was aware that there were poor drivers on the road, and I was hoping not to run into one. I passed the time by singing songs in Kurdish, Turkish, Azeri, and Arabic. I left Sacramento and reached the California-Nevada border, and ran into twisting and curving roads and lots of snow. I felt a responsibility to drive safely though, to protect myself so that I could continue to take care of my wife and dear boys.

I feared the snowstorms and dangerous driving conditions. I would slow down, but then speed up to get away from a potential snow avalanche as quickly as possible. The windshield became covered with ice, and I thought the windshield washer tank was empty. I stopped to get gas, and I bought some antifreeze for the windshield washer tank, but it was frozen over, and I couldn't fill the tank. I removed the ice from the windshield and continued down the road.

Nighttime came, and I passed a huge truck just before entering a tunnel. Then the truck behind me passed me, ignoring the speed limit, and it suddenly turned in front of me, throwing dust, sand, and gravel at

288

my new car. I slowed down; I wanted to maintain control of the car. The truck then speeded away.

I drove along mountain roads and reached Reno, Nevada. I enjoyed the colorful, bright lights, even though I was tired. I listened to the car radio from time to time, and learned about the primary election results, the contest between Barak Obama and Hillary Clinton. I continued through the Nevada desert and finally reached the Utah border. The road was slippery and bleak, and I had to be careful. I did not want to plunge into a lake. I was driving behind a truck, because I knew that the driver knew the road and would help me if I got into an emergency situation. So I kept driving on the salty road until I reached a service area. I stopped for gas and food, but could not clear the ice from my windshield. I ran the engine for about ten minutes to heat the car, and I cleared a circular spot that allowed me to see the road. I then got back on I-80 East and reached Salt Lake City.

It was 3:00 a.m., but I didn't stop there. It was snowing, and I thought about my wife and sons in Lakeville. They had no idea I was driving through the Utah Mountains, breaking the speed limit, even though my windshield was not fully cleared. I felt that I had super strength, and the danger seemed to give me some sense of pleasure. I was still peering through a clearing in the windshield, about five inches in diameter. I had to bend forward to see the road ahead.

I left Utah and entered Wyoming, passing the spot where I had been given a speeding ticket on

289

December 13, 2007. The snow was still a problem, and at about 3:30 a.m. I decided to get a hotel room, to get some rest and get out of the snow.

I awoke at 6:00 a.m., took a shower and had breakfast, and then again hit the still snowy road. I was moving down the mountain sides, driving slowly and enjoying the sight. The weather had turned cold, but the car heater was working, sometimes the car would slide left and right and I saw cars and trucks that had crashed. I was going up mountains and down mountains, driving along curving roads, and occasionally listening to the radio. I had no CDs, so I had no music. I was driving carefully and day dreaming at the same time. But it was tough driving, given the windshield problem, cold weather, and snowy roads.

I reached Nebraska and saw variety kinds of vehicles that had slipped off the icy roads. The darkness and the snow prevented me from continuing, and I found a small hotel. I felt like writing a letter to the Nebraska governor and telling him about the poor condition icy roads, but decided to just have dinner.

I awoke early on the morning of December 14 and took a hot shower, trying to erase the images of crashed vehicles I had seen the previous day, but they wouldn't go away. Then my heart and breathing began to act strangely. I called the front desk and said, "I am on my bed, and it feels like I'm having heart attack. Would you please call emergency services?" The clerk thought I was kidding, but then he heard my odd breathing, and he made the call.

The police arrived accompanied by the medical team, who checked my chest and said I was OK. They told me that two days of driving on dangerous roads without sufficient rest or sleep can make one sick. I thanked them and showed them my health insurance card, but they said that there would be no charge. God bless America. Yes, my family and I always appreciate being in America.

I went down to the lobby and had some bread and orange juice, then found a gas station, but it was too early in the morning to find a mechanic and to get my windshield problem taken care of. I resumed my journey, crossing Nebraska and coming into Iowa, where I located two mechanics. They said, "We have to let your car stay inside the shop for few hours or until ice in the windshield washer container melts"

I did not like this idea. Then they told me that the cost would be $90, and I didn't like that either. As I prepared to leave, I asked what I owed, and they said that there was no charge. I got back on the road and finally reached Minnesota. I reached my house in Lakeville, and everyone was happy to see me—dad was finally home.

We celebrated the New Year, 2008. On January 4, while driving my son's car, I was hit by another car, a consequence of poor traffic signs. No one was injured, but the car was totaled. I complained to the Apple Valley mayor's office, but did not get any response. I was due to resume my teaching duties in Monterey on June 22, but we were not happy about it. We were not able to enjoy spring and summer breaks, as we were when I was teaching in public schools.

Ch. 29- Taha: A Linguist in Iraq (2008-2010)

In April of 2008, I resigned from the Defense Language Institute and applied for a job with the Global Linguist Solutions (GLS) Company. I completed their required tests over the phone, and my sons told me, "You need to relax; you don't have to work." I thanked them for their concern and said, "I want to work. I am able to work, and I want to make sure that Malika has health insurance for her diabetes problem. My sons understood the insurance issue, and they finally allowed me to take the job.

On November 21, 2008, I reported to the Minneapolis-St. Paul airport with Malika. It was a sad goodbye. Tears were dropping from her beautiful eyes onto her lovely cheeks. I told her that although I would be away for a time; my heart would always be with her. I flew to Atlanta and from there to Fort Benning, Georgia, arriving at 2:00 a.m. on a cold morning. I had previously spent time there in November of 2002, and I had my shower strategy worked out.

After six days of training, I flew to Kuwait, where I initially spent three days at Al-Salim airport, and then flew on to Balad Military Base in Iraq. After five days there, I flew on to Warhorse base by helicopter, and then on December 3, 2008, I joined a US Army military unit at the Jalawla Iraqi military base. I arrived on a dark and cloudy night at about 1:30 a.m. I was greeted by a group of US Special Forces troops, each with a flashlight, and they showed me the way to my quarters.

293

We were not allowed to use electrics light for fear of being bombed. The base was located between the cities of Jalawla and Saadia cities in Iraq. The unit was a small part of the Iraqi military base called Jalawla.

Taha with Special Forces in Jalawla/ Iraq

Early the next morning, I reported to the unit office, met my point of contact person (POC), and got my work orders. The unit's main gate and two towers were guarded by Kurdish freedom fighters (Peshmerga). The unit had no chow hall—and no PX, BX, library, or post office—but plenty of food: meat, bread, vegetables, fruits and nuts, pistachios, peanuts. Water and soda supplies were available. The unit had a small kitchen and one cook, who prepared food for about twenty soldiers.

The Peshmergas were Kurdish fighters, and I was told I would be having lunch and supper with them. They were very respectful and hospitable. They all greeted me warmly and helped carry my bags to my prepared room—my second American home.

I began carrying out my duties as a translator, translating from both sides, American and Iraqi. I did not carry a weapon, but I went along on military operations in the plains, mountains, and valleys—sometimes in the rain and cold. At age 65, I found I would sometimes develop painful knees. I especially admired the commander of US forces, a captain who listened closely to my advice. I tried to explain to each side of US military and Iraqi the differences in their cultures.

After six months of work with these Special Forces troops, I asked the captain to transfer me to a fixed military unit so I could do my translation inside a camp.

He provided me a report on May 1st, 2009, and dated it 30 May 2009, which allowed me to count my upcoming month of vacation in America as a duty time with Special Forces.

UNITED STATES DEPARTMENT OF DEFENSE

30 May 2009

MEMORANDUM FOR RECORD

SUBJECT: Recommendation for Taha M. Muhammad

1. Mr. Muhammad has worked under my supervision during combat operations in support of Operation Iraqi Freedom as an interpreter for five months.

2. During those five months, Mr. Muhammad proved himself invaluable part of my unit. His efforts directly impacted the effectiveness and efficiency of our operations. On a daily basis he performed a variety of duties. He routinely served as an interpreter for my detachment during meetings with Iraqi officers and soldiers from the Iraqi Army, Police, and the Kurdish security forces, politicians, tribal Shayikhs from Arab, Kurd, and Turkoman tribes, and civilians from all segments of society. He also maintained contact with these senior Iraqi leaders during nightly phone conversations. Another of his daily duties was in translating documents into English or Arabic. He translated over 200 documents during five months. On a daily basis, Mr. Muhammad worked with Iraqi contractors, and was essential to the ordering and receiving of over $140,000 worth of goods and services.

3. Mr. Muhammad was diligent and conscientious in performing all of these duties, always willing to work as a member of a team and following his instructions to the limit of his ability. His hard work was an important part of the unit's success for over five months of counter-insurgency operations.

William Harris
CPT, SF
Commander

Special Force Recommendation May 5, 2009

295

Vacation to America, May 5, 2009
I got permission from my army unit and the L-3 Linguist Company to return to America for a one-month vacation. I arrived at the Minneapolis-St. Paul airport, where I was greeted by my family members, who escorted me to our home in Lakeville. While in Minnesota, I made an appointment with a clearance officer to get my final secret clearance (CAT II). I obtained it and was ready to return to Iraq.

Back to Iraq
On June 5, 2009, my family again dropped me off at the Minneapolis-St. Paul airport, and again Malika was so sad to see me go. I retraced my steps, and after a twelve-hour flight, my huge plane landed in Kuwait. We reached Balad the next day, and Warhorse three days later, where I met my new GLS manager—a smart, respectful, and diplomatic man. Several days later, he informed me that I had been assigned to Q-West base in Iraq. His assistant manager gave me a ride to Warhorse airport, and from there I flew by helicopter to Tikreet base, and then a day later to Q-West in Iraq.

Taha: linguist in Q-West in Iraq
I arrived in Q-west on June 29, 2009, and reported to the linguist office and arranged to meet the military unit's point of contact (POC) person. That afternoon, the POC and another linguist moved my bags to that linguist Chu (room), and I was told I would be staying with him. I was disappointed. He had been a cigarette smoker for many years and had continued the

296

habit. In a matter of days, my chest began to ache, and I felt that I should ask for a Chu for myself. I didn't want to offend my new linguist colleague, who was being so friendly. I went to a military clinic to have my eyes examined, and when I went to register at the desk, I saw that my friend had followed me.

The clinic's clerk said, "Who is sick.

I said, "I am."

My colleague linguist said, "He is sick, but I am like his son." The clerk said OK, and she allowed my friend to remain with me, as he obtained my personal profile information. My friend started to follow me into the examination room, but I stopped him, and he agreed to wait for me in the lobby.

My colleague linguist's cigarette breath in the Chu (room) made me so tired. I went by myself to the housing office to persuade the director that I had a chest pain, caused by a person who was a heavy smoker. I said that the Chu was full of nicotine. One military person told me, "You are sick; we will return you to America."

I said, "I am not sick, but I need a Chu for myself, and I know many Iraqi linguists each had their own Chu. My demand did not work, and I came back to the nicotine filled Chu, without losing my job.

My linguist friend was a good person, and we spent a lot of time together, in the chow hall, at the gym, and at the local market.

Recommendation from Special Agent of USA Army

298

I stayed at Q-West base in Qayara, Iraq, for the next six months, as dust seemed to increasingly cloud my vision. My eyes turned red and then my vision became blurry, especially in my left eye, and I was advised to see an eye doctor. But the base had none available. My vision grew steadily worse, and I could do nothing but wait and complete my second six months. I finally requested a twenty-day vacation, which was approved.

Taha to America

I returned to America and made an appointment with an eye doctor, who recommended some surgery. He completed a medical report to show to my employer, and I spent some nice time with my family, shoveling snow and enduring the cold weather—quite a contrast. My family and I visited the Mall of America, and it was great to see people moving around freely and without fear. This is my wish for Iraq and the rest of the world— peace and prosperity for all.

Taha back to Iraq, January 28, 2010

I was prepared to return to my job at Q-West, but my point of contact (POC) person e-mailed me and notified me that they had moved to Mosul. My family saw me off at the airport again, and four flights later I reached the Mosul military base in Iraq. My POC met me, as did my friend, and fortunately the Mosul base had an eye clinic. The doctor looked at my medical report and examined both eyes, and then wrote a report recommending that I return to America for eye surgery.

My employer, L-3 Company, gave me a medical leave that allowed me to address my eye and knee problems. I made an appointment with an eye surgeon, Jeff Sanderson. On March 16, 2010, I left Mosul, flew to Balad, then to Kuwait, and from there to America. On March 26, Dr. Sanderson performed successful surgery on both eyes. While recovering in Minnesota, my job ended—the military to which I had been assigned had completed its Iraq assignment. I applied to the Minnesota job services office for unemployment income.

Our health insurance from L-3 Linguist Company was still in force, since I was on medical leave. After a few weeks, I recovered my health, and began to help around the house, shoveling snow, mowing grass, and going shopping.

All in all, I felt good about having been a part of the U.S. military effort, serving as an Iraqi and American interpreter, and teaching at the Defense Language Institute. I met thousands of soldiers and dozens of leaders, all of whom demonstrated great qualities of humanity, courage, and dignity. I am also proud of my new country, America. I am proud of the ways that Americans provide humanitarian aid, always ready to assist refugees and poor people, and to rebuild damaged communities.

I always write letters to the White House, to senators, and to the speaker of the House of Representatives. I began writing some books, and I worked at renewing my math teaching license. I was also prepared to teach Arabic, Kurdish, and Turkish. I resumed my painting, and I was always ready to help my neighbors.

I am proud to represent Kurdistan, and I cherish this letter from the Kurdistan Regional Government in the U.S.:

Kurdistan Regional Government—USA 2:19 PM

To: T M
From: US KRG (us@krg.org).
Sent: Thu 4/23/15 2:19 PM
To: T M (thmson@hotmail.com)

Dear Mr. Muhammad,

Thank you very much for your message. It is a very timely one, as the Kurdistan Regional Government is actively working to pass a resolution acknowledging the crimes against the Kurds.

Again, thank you very much for your support. We will be in touch with ways that you can take action and help, and we very much appreciate your interest!

Best Regards,

Kurdistan Regional Government - Iraq
Representation in the United States

I sent this letter to the US government:

1532 16th Street N.W.
Washington, D.C. 20036 USA

My family and I escaped from the brutal Saddam regime. We found freedom in America, and I was able to earn bachelor and master degrees in mathematics. This achievement would have been impossible in Saddam's Iraq. I did not belong to the Ba'ath Party, and I had no influence with them. In America, I was able to acquire a nice house. My wife, Malika is getting the best medical care for her diabetes, and my other family members are happy. We are going to do our best to go forward, and to help others, as others have helped us.

We are a father and mother extremely proud of our sons who got their education and gathered important degrees as pharmacist Doctor, computer network engineering, and International and Political Studies. We are very proud and honored that we are a veteran family. My son Cameron served in USA Army for 16 years. We are honored that three sons in our family members were linguists with USA troops in Iraq. Our lives were endangering as well as USA military personals at Iraq War.

My wife, Malika, published her book "Mama Malika's Iraqi Cookbook" in English version and also in Arabic Version. I made at home in Lonsdale storage, fence, and staircase. I published a few books in English version and Arabic.

We are very happy to be in America and to have the inner peace. God bless America the most humane country on the face of the Earth.

My Grand Daughter Lilly

Taha and his Fiction and Non-Fiction Books
New Prague Senior High School October 2016

October 20016, Taha Gives Presentation at Prior Lake
Senior Center in Minnesota

Honorable President Letter to Taha by E-mail
1/17/2017

The White House <info@mail.whitehouse.gov>

Yesterday, 2:39 PM
Tue 1/17/2017 2:39 PM

One of the most important things I've done as President is read messages from Americans like you. And whether you sat down to write me a letter back in 2009 or just last week, I wanted to say thank you for writing.
Letters like yours have given me the chance to hear the real stories that make up the ever changing narrative of America. They are stories of your setbacks and successes, your fears and your hopes not just for today—but for the country and the world we'll leave to our children and our grandchildren. I want you to know that I was listening. I heard your stories. And you made me a better President.
In 2014, a young mom took a chance and shared her family's story with me. She said she knew that "staying silent about what you see and what needs changing never makes any difference." She was right. And so, while serving you has been the greatest privilege of my life, I want you to know that when I leave the White House, I'll still hold the most important title of all: that of citizen.
And as a proud American citizen, I believe that we are a constant work in progress. Our success has never been certain. None of our journey has been preordained.

There's always been a gap between our highest ideals and the reality we witness every day. But what makes us exceptional—what makes us Americans—is that we have fought wars, and passed laws, and reformed systems, and organized unions, and staged protests, and launched mighty movements to close that gap. To bring the promise and the practice of America into closer alignment. To form that more perfect union.

So our collective future depends on our collective willingness to uphold our duties as citizens: to vote, to speak out, and to stand up for others knowing that each of us is only here because somebody, somewhere, stood up for us. And for the rest of my days, I promise I will be right there alongside you, continuing to do my part to build a better, more prosperous, more diverse and inclusive America—an America with a future full of hope.

From all of us in the Obama family—thank you for writing.

All the best,

Barack Obama

My E-mail to Honorable President Barak Obama

On 1/18/2016, My Reply:
Thank you very much Honor President Barack Obama for your letter to me (Taha M. Muhammad, the author of "We Survived Iraq and Turkey".
God bless you and your family and America.

US Kurdish citizen and humble Author
Taha M. Muhammad

The End
2017

Author
Taha M. Muhammad
US Kurdish Citizen